SILENCE

THE

ART

OF

STILLNESS

CHRIS KORNAROS

SILENCE

Silence: The Art of Stillness
Copyright © 2022 Chris Kornaros

All rights reserved.

No part of this publication may be reproduced in a retrieval system, or transmitted in any form or by any means—electronic, mechanical, photocopying, recording, or otherwise—without the prior written permission of the publisher.

This manuscript has undergone viable editorial work and proofreading, yet human limitations may have resulted in minor grammatical or syntax-related errors remaining in the finished book. The understanding of the reader is requested in these cases. While precaution has been taken in the preparation of this book, the publisher and author assume no responsibility for errors or omissions, or for damages resulting from the use of the information contained herein.

Scriptures taken from the Holy Bible, New International Version®, NIV®. Copyright © 1973, 1978, 1984, 2011 by Biblica, Inc.™ Used by permission of Zondervan. All rights reserved worldwide. www.zondervan.com The "NIV" and "New International Version" are trademarks registered in the United States Patent and Trademark Office by Biblica, Inc.™ Scripture taken from the New King James Version®. Copyright © 1982 by Thomas Nelson. Used by permission. All rights reserved. The Holy Bible, English Standard Version® (ESV®) Copyright © 2001 by Crossway, a publishing ministry of Good News Publishers. All rights reserved. ESV Text Edition: 2016. Scripture quotations marked (NLT) are taken from the Holy Bible, New Living Translation, copyright ©1996, 2004, 2015 by Tyndale House Foundation. Used by permission of Tyndale House Publishers, Carol Stream, Illinois 60188. All rights reserved. Scripture quotations taken from the Amplified® Bible (AMP), Copyright © 2015 by The Lockman Foundation. Used by permission. www.lockman.org. Scripture quotations marked TPT are from The Passion Translation®. Copyright © 2017, 2018 by Passion & Fire Ministries, Inc. Used by permission. All rights reserved. ThePassionTranslation.com. Scripture taken from the Contemporary English Version © 1991, 1992, 1995 by American Bible Society. Used by Permission.

This book is set in the typeface *Athelas* designed by Veronika Burian and Jose Scaglione.

Paperback ISBN: 978-1-955546-26-3

A Publication of *Tall Pine Books*
119 E Center Street, Suite B4A | Warsaw, Indiana 46580
www.tallpinebooks.com

| 1 22 22 20 16 02 |

Published in the United States of America

"The demands of being a wife, mother, and a small business owner leave little time for rest or reflection. This book is a great reminder and encouragement to slow down. Life can get so busy and it's hard to take time to hear the voice of God in all the chaos. *Silence: The Art of Stillness* was very well written. It is an easy read that will speak to your heart and serve as a reminder of what's really important."

Brooke Huffman
Owner, *The Social Sip*

"This is more than another book on introverts in the church. Extroversion as an excuse for why we can't be silent, still, or practice rest is a fallacy. If Jesus made it his priority, then it's a requirement for us to live outside and beyond the anxious trouble and persecution that Jesus prophesied for us. Chris is the only person I know that finds a back bedroom at a social gathering to take a 90-minute power nap. He practices what he preaches, to the astonishment of many. He's challenged me many times to be alone and vulnerable with Jesus, stare into His face and ask Him what His heart is for me. I'm telling you, Chris is telling us that Jesus is telling His heart for us: Be Still!"

Kris Rosentrater
Founder, *Clash Creative Ministries*

"As the world continues to feed the fast-paced-your-way-right-away lifestyle, the art of stillness and value of silence has been waning. *Silence: The Art of Stillness* is a timely reminder and provides practical tools for returning to peace and rest. Through the pages of Chris' story you will find strength to overcome any busyness or chaos in your life."

Sarah Crockett
Head of Digital Content, *GOD TV*

"The war over our flesh often lands in the conflict between busy-ness and rest, and stillness loses more often than not. Chris Kornaros' new book is an effective new tool for elevating the value and importance of regularly submitting our whole selves to the conversation God longs to have with us."

Robert Caggiano
Managing Editor, *Charisma Media*

CONTENTS

Foreword .... *xv*
Introduction .... *xvii*

1. What is Silence? 1
2. A Time for Silence 11
3. Pressing Through Awkward Silence 25
4. Silencing Busyness 39
5. Silence and Inner Stress 51
6. Silence and External Stressors 65
7. Finding Clarity 77
8. Being at Rest 97
9. Recalibration 111
10. God Speaks Through People 119
11. Silence is Golden 131
12. Lingering with God 141
13. Cultivating Intimacy 153
14. Leaving a Legacy 161
15. Jesus and Silence 171

Conclusion *179*

Footnotes *181*
Acknowledgements *188*
About the Author *191*

To Sean,
You unknowingly taught me how to listen well to others,
But mostly to the Father.
I love you brother, I will see you again face to face in glory.

"To You belongs silence [the submissive wonder of reverence], and [it bursts into] praise in Zion, O God;" – Psalm 65:1 AMP

FOREWORD

Silence: The Art of Stillness is an invitation to an important dimension of a healthy life that is often overlooked in a culture of noise and constant activity. The unending social media opportunities for interaction have short-circuited our time and the quality of intimacy with our family and friends. The time of rest in silence is under siege by digital media. The informational overload in this generation is deteriorating our mental health as a nation. We must choose to be silent. Recapturing our quiet time before Father God adds strength to everything we do. This book empowers our spiritual life with practical applications to build a time of meditation before the Lord. It includes a short prayer, activation for silence, and a takeaway thought to bring a focus at the end of each chapter. An unusual peace came over me as I was reading his book in the middle of my busy schedule. I realized that I needed to schedule additional silence in God's presence.

Chris Kornaros has insights and truths through his

personal walk that helps us develop a more intimate relationship with God and friends through the strength of silence. The effectiveness of the ministry of Jesus was based in His personal quiet time with Father God. In the scriptures, 1 Peter 3:4 reminds us of the "incorruptible beauty of a gentle and quiet spirit." Silence brings His beauty into our lives. Live beautifully in a broken world. It brings hope to those we meet.

–Dr. Dale L. Mast
Pastor, International Speaker, Bible School Teacher
Author: *And David Perceived He Was King, Two Sons and A Father, The Throne of David, Shattering the Limitations of Pain.*

INTRODUCTION

In 2018 our family of four made a significant move to Austin, Texas and purchased a new house to call home. One month after settling in I was in the garage painting an old dresser I'd found on Craigslist because it smelled as if it had been around since the 1970s.

When I took a break and went inside the house to get a snack, my wife mentioned to me she had missed multiple calls from a close friend. We called her back. Being a trained nurse, our friend delivered her news without any fluff, in a straightforward manner: "He is dead." Her husband, one of my closest childhood friends, had passed away.

I was in shock. No words came: what was there to say? I could only choke out, "Oh man, I'm so sorry!" As my wife continued talking with our friend on the phone I went outside to call some of our mutual close friends and share the news with them. We mourned together our traumatic and sudden loss.

Not knowing what else to do after hearing such tragic

news, I continued painting the dresser. Like most people, I wasn't trained for shock and trauma: it just happened and needed to be worked out. So in my numbness I went through the motions of busy-work for the rest of the day.

Over the course of the next three weeks I woke up disillusioned, depressed, and confused. After shuffling out to my morning coffee and breakfast, I had no ability to muster energy for anything other than going back to bed.

At the time I was on a yearlong sabbatical. Though I didn't realize it then, having that space and time in my schedule afforded me the privilege of fully processing the loss we were all experiencing. Had I been working, I would have been distracted with the day-to-day demands of the job, and sorting out the effects of my friend's death would've occurred more quickly. As a result, I believe my processing would've been incomplete.

Through this time of sabbatical, after the upheaval of moving to a new city and the pain of deep loss, I came to understand what was important in my life. Insignificant details fell to the side. I often found myself on my recliner, lying there in silence.

It's interesting how tragedy and loss can bring perspective. Up until that period in my life I'd been quite effective at distracting myself with projects and menial tasks to avoid dealing with pain and facing it head on. But during that time of processing I started to see my life through the healthy focus of a new lens. I began to understand how much I needed silence in order to sort out my life, hear my own thoughts, and hear God's thoughts over me.

Almost a year after that deep time of working through the death of my friend, I was flying back home from a conference in the Seattle area. <u>After boarding the plane I turned off the monitor in front of me, decompressed, focused, and calibrated to connect with God. A few hours into the flight I heard this in my heart: "I want you to write a book on the art of silence."</u>

Since I hadn't written a book before, I didn't know where to start, so I did nothing. Three months later a friend gave me an encouraging word that illuminated what she saw inside of me—things I'd been unable to see myself. On the strength of her encouragement, and in obedience to what God had asked of me, I wrote these pages you are now reading.

I pray my journey with silence will encourage, uplift, edify, and strengthen you. My desire is that in these pages you will discover and unlock the beauty and soul-freeing moments silence can bring. I look forward to hearing from some of you to find out what you applied, what encouraged you, and how God showed up in your life because of *Silence!*

Blessings,
Chris Kornaros

CHAPTER ONE
WHAT IS SILENCE?

"Silence is so freaking loud." [1] – *Sarah Dessen*

I was once at an extremely loud concert. Everyone around me was screaming at the top of their lungs. The noise in the stadium was so deafening I could hardly think. There was frenzied energy all around me as the crowd crammed and pressed rather violently. I got caught in the middle of the crush of people flowing forward, thrusting me toward the front. With so many bodies pushing close, I started to sweat profusely; the air became thin and I began to have trouble breathing.

Security guards stood at the front of the crowd behind four-foot-high crowd-control metal bars. They were holding the bars up and pulling people out who were being smashed into the bars by the force of the crowd. I was able to work my way to the front and have the guards pull me out of the surrounding madness. After escaping the crowd, it took me thirty minutes to regain my composure.

Sometimes life can appear this way. Pressures and stress can build up to the point that we're forced to remove ourselves from what's happening in order to regain composure. In the concert situation I had to escape from the pressing crowd and find room to breathe. <u>The same is true for our spiritual and emotional health; sometimes we need to remove ourselves from the pressing crowd of people, details, and demands, and give ourselves room to breathe.</u>

That's what this book is about. Through my own life experiences I'll share how silence is used by God to change us, heal us, and build a relationship with us. When I speak of silence I'm not referring only to a lack of sound, but to the life qualities of quiet and solitude that have become invaluable to me.

The Many Forms of Silence

Silence can take many different forms. The shape of my silence will be unique from one time to another. One time it could look like <u>purposeful prayer.</u> Another time it <u>could be taking a nap, or going on a walk and conversing with God, or sitting quietly with my thoughts. Whatever it looks like, healthy silence will lead us toward God.</u>

I love how author Henri Nouwen describes silence.

He writes that it is "The discipline by which the inner fire of God is tended and kept alive."[2] When I think about tending a fire, I have to give it my attention and cultivate it to keep it lit. Pursuing silence is a key for discovering and maintaining intimacy with God.

Silence is referred to as a *spiritual discipline*. A spiritual discipline is a practice that brings us closer to God. There are many other spiritual disciplines that are perhaps more familiar to us, including practices like prayer, fasting, worship, serving, and fellowship.

Solitude, defined as the state of being alone [3], is also known to be a spiritual discipline. We often see these two words in tandem as *silence and solitude,* since the two disciplines are related. The ultimate example of solitude is when Jesus retreated from the crowds to be alone with His Father, to pray and hear what He was speaking. It goes without saying that in this book, we'll discuss the importance of both disciplines.

Silence in spirituality is often a metaphor for *inner stillness*. A silent mind, freed from an onslaught of thoughts and thought patterns, is both a goal and an important step in spiritual development. Such *inner silence* is not about the absence of sound. Instead, it is understood to bring us in contact with the Divine and Ultimate Reality, and to connect us with our true self and our divine nature. Many religious traditions believe in the importance of being quiet and still in mind and spirit in order for transformative and integral spiritual growth to occur. [4]

Internal silence is learning to quiet the noises inside our heads and hearts so we can hear God. It is priceless. Its valuable counterpart, *external* silence, has to do with removing all sound from around us to help us focus. I'll discuss both types of silence as I share my journey of finding intimacy and rest through the world of quietude.

Another form of silence is an action that is not passive in nature, but intentional. It's when I purposefully seek to communicate with God from my heart, but with no words from my lips. It includes speaking directly from my heart to His heart wherever I am, at any time of day. There are times when my heart brings Him praise through my lips, and there are times my heart brings Him praise through my silence (Psalm 65:1, 2; Hebrews 13:15). Silence is the small "Thank you" to God that fills my heart during the week: thanks for my health, my family, for His love and blessings. This fulfills what Paul wrote when he instructed us through the Holy Spirit to, "Rejoice always, pray continually, give thanks in all circumstances; for this is God's will for you in Christ Jesus" (1 Thessalonians 5:16-18, NIV). These don't always have to be done with words; they can also spring up from our hearts in silence.

One more form of silence is its power to create life. A study was done in 2013 with mice. The study compared their behaviors during two different scenarios. In the first scenario the mice were exposed to different noises. For the second scenario the mice were immersed in pure silence. The scientists observed when the mice were exposed to two hours of silence per day, new cells developed in the hippocampus, the part of the brain known to have memory, emotion, and learning. <u>Silence afforded the creation of new cells, and those new cells became a functioning part of the brain, literally *growing the brain.*</u> [5]

In modern society we are surrounded by noise pollution, and it does more damage than we think. Studies have shown that noise affects our stress levels by raising cortisol and adrenaline levels in our bodies. And yet, with only two minutes of silence, we can relieve pressure. <u>Silence is more relaxing for our bodies than listening to music. Silence helps lower blood pressure and brings about an increase of blood flow to the brain.</u> [6]

I marvel at people who can accomplish anything while sitting at a café, working on their computers and listening to music on their headphones. All around them is a stimulating environment with movement, sound, and relational conversations. Their workplaces are full of visual and auditory noise.

Right now I'm sitting at my desk, writing in relative silence. My wife is watching a show on her computer in a distant room. The only added sound is the falling of light rain outside my window.

Silence is so beautiful!

But if we are not in love with silence, as Sarah Dessen noted, silence may seem "so freaking loud" to us, like that rock concert I attended as a young adult. Now, I'm not implying sitting in silence is easy. There are many times I don't want to sit in silence. Yet more often than not, sitting in silence is exactly what I *need*.

I am naturally a doer. I enjoy projects and getting things accomplished and feeling the satisfaction of having completed something. To sit alone with my thoughts has not been my go-to discipline. It used to be the last thing I wanted to do with my time. But I have learned its benefits over the years. And now, sitting in silence has become an ally. I know the demands of life will continue to pull at me from every direction. But just as doing His Father's will was Jesus' food (John 4:34), so silence has become spiritual food for me.

I hope it will become nourishment for you, too.

Convergence of Love

I was praying one day and asked the Lord, "Show me something about silence." What I heard in my heart was, *Silence is the convergence of contagious love.* That statement didn't immediately make sense to me, so I pondered it for a while, and that led to researching the meaning of convergence.

Convergence is "When two or more things come together to form a new whole, like the convergence of plum and apricot genes in the plumcot." [7] Convergence comes from the prefix *con*, meaning *together*, and the verb *verge*, which means *to turn toward*. It also means "When two paths come together and form one path."

The Lord was saying when I sit in silence before Him, we are *together,* and we are *turning toward one another.* He and I are becoming one. We are grafting into each other. When I come to Him in silence and we are communing, He is infectiously filling me with His DNA of love.

God wants to fill each of us with His infectious love (1 John 4:7). We need to give Him our quiet focus and create time for Him to do so. When we take time to still our souls to be with Him, He fills us with His DNA of love, which can then become contagious inside and outside of us. His love becomes contagious *inside* of us as He fills our hearts, as we sense the reality of the cross, as we sense His goodness toward us. It becomes contagious *outside* of us, because what He has poured into our hearts cannot be contained. It leaks onto everyone we come in contact with, as written in Jeremiah 20:9 (NIV): "His word is in my heart like a fire, a fire shut up in my bones. I am weary of holding it in; indeed, I cannot." This love that comes to us through convergence in our silence with God is contagious.

Avoiding Silence

There are many reasons we avoid silence; many things that keep us from appreciating silence. Giving space to silence can almost feel threatening. It's possible some of us have so much inner noise in our heads, we find it hard to pause or think clearly. The noise can be so loud, we have a hard time filtering what is from God, from us, or from another source. So we try to drown it out by filling our lives with activity. For others, being surrounded by noise is all we've known: it's the only way we have experienced life. And for many of us, the idea of sitting alone with our thoughts is the scariest thing in the world because we've ignored facing past hurts, abuses, tragedies, or pains, and we don't want to give them the opportunity to surface during the quiet moments.

The only way we will be able to conquer the noise in our lives is by accepting the healing power of silence. Silence is the entryway into a new world. Silence opens many doors to our hearts and allows healing and rest to occur (Psalm 62:5). Silence allows God to come and meet us with His contagious, unifying, fiery love. Silence is our ally.

Pray this prayer:

Lord, I want to meet with you. I want you and I to become one. I choose to create moments of silence with you. Be in my heart like a fire, like a fire that cannot be contained. Teach me the ways of silence. May I eagerly desire it and long for it. I love you, Jesus. Amen.

Activation:

Take a few minutes and sit in silence. Clear your mind and think only about God's love for you.

Takeaway:

Silence brings love to us through the convergence of God's presence and my presence with Him. Silence tends the inner fire of God in us. It is an inner stillness that creates life. Silence is our ally.

CHAPTER 2
A TIME FOR SILENCE

"The monotony and solitude of a quiet life stimulates the creative mind."[1] Albert Einstein

When I was growing up my mother instituted quiet times in the mornings. We would have to spend one hour in our room playing, reading, or doing whatever we could do to pass the time. As children we often felt trapped. We waited, begged, and called from our rooms every ten or fifteen minutes: "Is it time to come down yet?" Ten minutes at that stage in my life felt like hours! Some days I really hated that quiet hour because being isolated in my room wasn't my first choice for an activity. But on other days I loved it, enjoying the quiet of playing or reading by myself.

Now that I'm a parent, I realize why my mother made us have quiet time; it was because SHE needed quiet time from her two high-energy boys! I laugh about it now, but I have established the same habit with my children. And now they are asking the same question, "Can we come out of our room now?"

I recently heard a saying that when kids claim they are bored it is a good thing, because boredom actually stimulates their minds to create and use their imagination!

As I mentioned before, I've discovered silence is my friend, my ally, and not an enemy. It has become for me a source of solace, rest, and comfort. This foe I was forced to spend time with as a child is now one of my closest companions.

Apportioning Time

Despite the busyness of work, family, and life, my wife and I love to travel. We make it a priority in our schedule. Another priority for us is hosting people in our home. We thoroughly enjoy firing up the grill for an evening of barbeque or playing games with friends. Prioritizing space and time in our lives for what we love to do enables us to live joyfully. And joy is an essential aspect of daily life in the Kingdom of God (See the Bible: Nehemiah 8:10, Galatians 5:22, 1 Timothy 6:17).

Along with our family's priorities of travel and hosting friends, I have added the personal priority of *silence*.

Because of the value it adds to my life, I've chosen to place more importance on times of silence than on other aspects of my schedule. Walking out that decision now as an adult has been a learning process of discovery and healing. When I first put silence on my sacred list of what takes precedence, it created some real challenges. I had to forego social gatherings because I knew my soul needed rest. I had to stop filling my schedule with more events and activities. Reversing the pattern of filling up my calendar was—and still is—an ever-present battle. But in terms of the benefits gained, I have found *less is more*.

If we spend too much time in one area of our life, the other areas of our life will suffer. There is a Kingdom rhythm and balance for the time we spend in each area of our lives that, with God's help, only we can figure out and walk out.

For example, we've all heard the phrase, "Time is money." As a kid, this saying made no sense to me. It was only as I grew older and started working for myself that those words took on meaning. I entered the working world as a self-employed contractor and set strict financial goals to pay off college loans, my cars, and my house—all of which I have since achieved. When I first started out, I set a goal to make $100,000 in sales in one year. I thought when I hit that financial goal I would feel better about myself and feel more accomplished. But meeting that goal only produced in me a pressure to one-up myself and make even *more* money.

I've since discovered, as much as I need money to live, I also need *time* to be able to live a quality life. I have personally adjusted the phrase from "Time is money," to "Time is more valuable to me than money." Rather than needing added overtime, I need *extra quality time* to be with those I love, and for doing the things I enjoy.

So I've made some changes. Instead of sitting in rush-hour traffic on the interstate every day, I take the toll road to and from work. I've chosen to pay the toll for the extra hour I get to spend with my family. I have realized by doing this, I'm making better use of my time.

I grew up hearing a song called *Turn! Turn! Turn!* by The Byrds. The lyrics are from the book of Ecclesiastes in the Bible, which was written by a wise king named Solomon. I've chosen to print the entire passage about *time* here because of the poetic truth it presents.

Even if it's a familiar passage, take a moment to read it as if it's the first time you're hearing it. Consider what it speaks about time and its value:

There is a time for everything,
and a season for every activity under the heavens:
a time to be born and a time to die,
a time to plant and a time to uproot,
a time to kill and a time to heal,
a time to tear down and a time to build,
a time to weep and a time to laugh,

a time to mourn and a time to dance,
a time to scatter stones and a time to gather them,
a time to embrace and a time to refrain from embracing,
a time to search and a time to give up,
a time to keep and a time to throw away,
a time to tear and a time to mend,
a time to be silent and a time to speak,
a time to love and a time to hate,
a time for war and a time for peace.

What do workers gain from their toil? I have seen the burden God has laid on the human race. He has made everything beautiful in its time. He has also set eternity in the human heart; yet no one can fathom what God has done from beginning to end. (Ecclesiastes 3:1-11 NIV)

I love this passage! It brings us back to the takeaway for this section: if we spend too much time in one area of our lives, the other areas will suffer. We bring order to the larger picture of our lives by discerning how much time to spend in each area, and by understanding, with God's wisdom, what season of life we're in, and how to best divide our time in each season.

Consider another popular phrase of our culture: "Work hard, play hard." A few years ago my wife and I played hard on a three-week trip to Europe. We wanted to get a taste of many different cities and not miss anything! Because we wanted to see it all, we packed our schedule as full as an overstuffed suitcase.

In hindsight, we really needed twice the amount of allotted time for all the sightseeing we fit into our schedule. Our crammed agenda created a lot of stress and pressure. We were playing hard, but there was no time to rest! We didn't need that kind of "play" during our vacation! We needed time to breathe and to enjoy, to rest and to refresh.

From that experience we learned not to fill playtime—travel and vacations—full of activity. Now when we travel, we allow additional time to visit each city, and we also schedule in a few days of rest. There is a time for everything: a time for rest, a time for play, and a time for work. Solomon was right!

Families can spend so much time and money on vacations to have an experience. The assumption is that it's vacation, so of course it will be restful. But that isn't necessarily true, as our own whirlwind trip to Europe demonstrates. Some advice for vacations that aren't exhausting: set aside a few days of rest before and after the vacation. It'll help everyone enjoy the vacation time more. And as we learned, don't fill every moment with activities. Allowing time for rest will make the vacation more pleasant and relaxing.

A Time to Listen

While growing up, I talked more than I listened. I felt I had to have an answer for everything and let my opinions be known. I remember spending time with friends who had incredible listening skills. I spoke most of the time, and when it was their turn to share, rather than listening, I was thinking about the next thing I was going to say. I was a kid trying to find my voice. My need to be heard far outweighed the desire to listen and understand. With such an imbalance, I wasn't able to fully enjoy my relationships. I imagine my friends felt the same.

Richard Foster writes in his book *Celebration of Discipline*, that, "To listen to others quiets and disciplines the mind to listen to God."[2] Not being a skillful listener in my younger years later translated into my relationship with God and into my prayer life. I was effective at verbalizing my needs and desires to God but struggled with giving Him space to express His thoughts to me through the Holy Spirit. I was missing the incredible value of hearing God's voice and understanding His perspective, His viewpoint, and His feelings!

Since my teenage years, I've learned a few things about friendship and conversation. I now understand the importance of listening well. It's selfish when we don't listen well or when we only half listen to another person. I've learned to show honor and respect to those in my life by *listening actively* to understand, and my hope is that it is reciprocated.

Part of the beauty of learning to be silent is that we learn to listen more. Being silent for the sake of having the peace and rest of quiet stillness is priceless. But add to that the quality of listening in prayer and listening to others, and the value we've added to the relationships around us increases. And that goes for our relationship with our Creator. Listening brings great value to all relationships.

In this age of cell phones, tablets, and devices, listening is in danger of becoming a lost art. We've all experienced the insult of trying to have a conversation with someone who is constantly checking their phone. We've watched families sitting at restaurant tables, with every family member silently staring at a cell phone or a tablet. The disconnect is real. We can miss opportunities for quality conversations through giving more attention to emails, texts, and games on our devices. All of us can benefit by brushing up on our listening skills and choosing to give our attention to the person sitting across from us.

An article was written in the *Harvard Business Review* called "What Great Listeners Actually Do."[3] The article describes six different levels of listening. Not every conversation requires the highest level of listening, but all conversations benefit from greater focus and listening skills. As you examine these six levels, consider how they apply to your friendships, your family relationships, your work connections, people in your social circles, and even how they could apply to your friendship with God.

Level 1: The listener creates a safe environment in which difficult, complex, or emotional issues can be discussed.

Level 2: The listener removes distractions like cell phones, music, and laptops, and gives appropriate eye contact.

Level 3: The listener seeks to understand what is being said, asks questions, and restates what is being said to make sure their understanding is correct.

Level 4: The listener pays attention to nonverbal cues such as facial expressions, perspiration, respiration, gestures, posture, and other body language signals. Eighty percent of human communication comes from these signals, so it's important to "listen" with both our eyes and our ears.

Level 5: The listener understands the person's feelings, acknowledges them, and empathizes with and validates those feelings in a supportive, nonjudgmental way.

Level 6: The listener asks questions that clarify assumptions the other person holds, helping the other person to see the issue in a new light and possibly offering useful suggestions to the other person. A skillful listener will not take over the conversation and turn what they want to say into the subject of the discussion.

The same article included another study that showed effective listening was much more than just being silent. It was, as they called it, a *cooperative conversation*. As in level six above, giving feedback, asking questions, and making suggestions made listening more helpful to the speaker.

There is a marvelous story in Genesis 18 that describes a *cooperative conversation* between Abraham and God. The story begins when God informs Abraham of His decision to wipe a horribly wicked city off the face of the earth. Abraham bargains with God, asking Him a clarifying question about His decision. And God responds. Now Abraham could have settled for God's initial answer, but he didn't. Instead, to see how God will respond and what He will say, Abraham asks God to consider changing the terms.

This incredibly intimate back-and-forth dialogue between the God of the universe and one of His humans gives us insight into what is possible in our intimate friendship with our heavenly Father! The give-and-take in their dialogue messes with our theology! It pulls us out

Listening to God → Obeying → Dialoguing

of religion and pushes us into intimacy and friendship with God—which has been His goal for us all along. So we discover that praying and listening to God is one level of relationship. Obeying is another level. And dialoguing with God, as Abraham did, reflects an even deeper level of intimate friendship.

I tell my kids *ASK* all the time, "Did you know both Abraham and Moses changed God's mind? (Exodus 32, Genesis 18)" While they're young, I want my children to know friendship with God is normal: that they have access to the Father and can dialogue with Him as a friend. I explain to them that the Father, Jesus and the Holy Spirit are their friends, because Jesus called His disciples friends rather than servants (John 15:15).

Choosing to Listen to God

Once, during a prayer time, when I closed my eyes, I saw a picture of Jesus putting His right hand on my heart and His left hand on my back. His head was bowed, as if He was praying for me. Then, out of His cloak, coming from His heart, appeared a pair of what looked like white Apple brand headphones. The headphones went into my ears and the vision ended.

I knew intuitively that while Jesus was praying for my heart, He was also releasing the *sound of His heart* into my ears, the sound of heaven. Each day we choose the sounds we will listen to and allow to influence us. We can

Each day, we choose which sounds →

listen to the sound of television, the sound of our phone, the sound of our computer, the sound of music, or no sound at all. We are bombarded daily with *things* that try to take our time and simultaneously put their sound into us, whether it be actual audible noise or emotional and mental noise from the world around us.

Whose voice are you listening to? There are voices of our past that speak to us. The voices of our friends and the voices of media speak to us. There are voices in our thoughts that create negative or positive self-talk. And there is God's voice. His voice is the most precious sound we could ever hear.

Pray this prayer:

Dec 2022
Prayer ♡

Jesus, I adore You. You are my center. I want to have a constant cooperative conversation with You. I pray my levels of listening will increase as my moments of speaking decrease. Help me see the beauty of silence and discover the amazing wonders it can bring to my life. May I begin to fully understand when it's time to speak and when it's time to be silent. May I listen for the sound of Your voice. I love You Jesus! Amen.

Activation #1:

From the six listening levels listed in this chapter, choose one aspect of listening you want to work on for the next

#1 Dec 12, 2022

WE WILL LISTEN TO.

month. Write it down on a Post-It Note and place it where you'll see it regularly. Begin applying that skill with people around you each day and see how your relationships grow as a result!

Activation #2:

Sometimes sitting quietly will help you process through life and think about things you may have put off doing, or discover things that are important to you that you haven't prioritized. Take a few quiet minutes and write down the first three things that pop into your head that are in your heart to do. Don't make excuses about why doing them won't work. Just write them down. Making them happen right away is not the goal. Writing them down will help you begin to recognize what is important to your heart and life.

Activation #3:

Take some time to reflect on how your relationship with God could become more of a dialogue than a one-way conversation.

Takeaway: ♡

Time for silence is important for your spiritual, emotional, and physical health and growth. Learning to listen well to both God and others will strengthen your relational connection with God. You can choose to listen for the sounds of heaven more than the sounds of earth.

CHAPTER 3
PRESSING THROUGH AWKWARD SILENCE

"Words were few and failing between them as though the silence that sat with them had laid its old lips on theirs and sucked them dry of speech." [1] – Michael Bedard

When I was eight years old my ten-year-old brother and I were always chasing each other around the house, either playfully, or as a result of fighting. When we were caught fighting my parents verbally disciplined us. Our response to their discipline was to laugh or cry because we could not emotionally process the intensity and the seriousness of the moment. We felt awkward, and for me personally, that emotion often elicited a humorous reaction.

We have all been there. We've all been at a loss for words and felt Awkward Silence steal into a conversation.

The big Awkward may have started when we got in trouble for doing something wrong and did not know how to respond; or when we got into a fight with a friend or a spouse, who asked us a question for which we had no reply. If we've not personally experienced the tension of Awkward Silence, we've certainly felt the pain of another person's loss for words.

When my daughter was seven and my son was five they performed a dragon show for my wife and me. They played theme music and pretended to be dragons. When my daughter saw us watching her, she suddenly became incredibly shy. Smiling broadly, she replied quietly, "I can't stop smiling!" She could not press through her shyness to finish the show. It was an awkward silence I could get used to, seeing her cute and adorable bashfulness.

Sometimes our human response to the Awkward Silence is to fill those uncomfortable spaces with words. We think by adding words to the silence—any words, even meaningless ones—we can fix the situation and cause the discomfort to vanish. But inevitably, these attempts can make things worse or prolong a conversation that should've ended five minutes earlier. Proverbs 10:19 (CEV) states it well: "You will say the wrong thing if you talk too much—so be sensible and watch what you say."

That was me in my younger years. I often handled conversational awkwardness by trying to use my words to fix a problem. But each time, I ended up verbally digging myself into a bigger hole instead of resolving tensions. It was as if my brain wasn't communicating with my mouth, because often what I *wanted* to say and what came out of my mouth were two different realities!

Solomon wrote in Ecclesiastes 5:1-3:

> *Guard your steps when you go to the house of God. Go near to listen rather than to offer the sacrifice of fools, who do not know that they do wrong. Do not be quick with your mouth, do not be hasty in your heart to utter anything before God. God is in heaven and you are on earth, so let your words be few. A dream comes when there are many cares, and many words mark the speech of a fool.*

James 1:19 also instructs us to "be quick to listen, slow to speak."

Essentially, these passages are saying that as we come before God, we're to listen more and not just fill that space with noise, words, activity, or our agenda. Our perceptions of God and of ourselves will inevitably negatively or positively affect our quiet times. If we tend to be doers, we may want to fill that time with activity. If we're schedulers, we might want to give God a specific amount of time. God can speak to us in spite of the parameters we set, but it may be better to approach times with Him as the writer of Lamentations 3:25-26 (NIV) directs us: "The Lord is good to those whose hope is in him, to the one who seeks him; it is good to wait quietly for the salvation of the Lord."

The problem with waiting is that sometimes we feel awkward with God. If we sit before Him and feel uncomfortable, it can shut us down. We might struggle to be ourselves with Him, but God wants us to push past the awkwardness. As our Father, God delights in seeing us and dialoguing with us.

How much of your quiet time with God is awkward? 20 percent? 80 percent? There may be a reason. The solution could be as simple as trying something new; moving to a new location; trying a different way of praying; or sitting in silence and speaking to God in your heart and mind without opening your mouth.

The Goodness of God

We may feel awkward with God because we've experienced life situations that have caused us to question His nature or His goodness. I'm so grateful my parents gave me a basis for personally understanding the goodness of God. As a kid, my parents reminded me of all that we had while growing up. We were told not to waste our food because there were kids around the world who barely had any food. Now I understand the world is larger than the United States, and as a first world nation, we have virtually everything we need at our disposal. But as a child, I only realized I was well taken care of when I met friends at school who had to look after themselves when they got home. And though my mom packed my lunch every morning, some of my friends had to make their own lunch. Even as a child, I could identify how blessed I was when I had something or someone to compare to my situation.

Later, as a twenty-something young adult, I was working with an audiovisual company at an event in Lake Tahoe, California. One day my dad left me a voicemail. He'd called to ask how I was doing and told me how much he loved me, adding that I was "his favorite boy." In the moment, I shared the voicemail message with my thirty-something friend, who immediately began to cry. When I saw someone deeply wishing for his own father to speak to him with loving words in the same way my dad had spoken to me, it impacted me. I then had a lens for understanding the goodness of my dad's fathering.

If you are reading this now and you weren't loved well or hugged enough; or you weren't told you are loved and that you're a handsome boy or a beautiful girl; if I were with you right now, I would give you a hug and speak those kinds of words over you! Even if your heart struggles to believe it, this is how God sees you, as handsome or beautiful, and as deeply loved.

God assures you through the prophet Jeremiah, *"Before you were in the womb I knew you" (Jer. 1:5)*. God has known you from eternity past and believes in you and loves you. You may not feel special or known right now, but God's got His eyes on you, beckoning you to come close! In Psalm 121:8, God promises, "The Lord will watch over your coming and going both now and forevermore."

The Goodness of God is Tested

But even with a good parental foundation that helped me grasp God's goodness, I have experienced times in life when I struggled to hold onto my faith in God's goodness. In the introduction of this book, I wrote about the shock I felt when hearing that my best friend had passed away. That season of grief and loss was the first time I wondered whether God was really good. I felt as if God had abandoned me.

God is all-knowing and all-powerful. But at the time of my friend's passing I wasn't able to wrap my mind around the fact that this loss was occurring within the scope of God's divine nature. Even though I had incredible reassurance in prayer, I still had to grapple with the tangible reality of trauma and loss. Did I really trust and believe in God's goodness? I wasn't sure, because my trust in His goodness had never been tested to that degree.

I sat in silence with God as I'd never done before. Though I didn't understand it then, my loss became an unforeseen gift that catapulted me into a new era of walking with God. The practice of silence I've written about in these pages became real during those days, weeks, and months. My loss became a thrusting point for diving deeper into my faith. In that time of grieving, I learned quickly that I needed God more than ever.

I also learned that I needed my friends to help me make it through that time. After having a prayer session with a close friend about my deep loss, I was overwhelmed with an incredible sense that not only was God with me, but that my best friend was with God.

In Christendom we are raised with an assumed belief in the goodness of God. But when circumstances come that test our beliefs, that assumed belief is challenged. Ultimately, to be connected in relationship with God, we have to believe He is good, or we'll struggle to relate to Him freely, without the awkwardness or anger that can interfere.

My goodness as a father to my children means I will do my best to love and protect them from danger and harm. But the decisions they make and the decisions made by those around them may affect them in ways I cannot control. But that doesn't mean I'm not present or that I have abandoned them. Life will happen, and when it does, I will always be ready to help when they come to me.

God's goodness doesn't mean life will always be perfect and comfortable and that everything will work out like we thought it would. He gives humans free will, and in a fallen world, not everyone around us will choose to use their free will in a healthy way. But God will be there to help us, keep us, restore us, and love us. He is a perfect Father who is passionately committed to growing His relationship with us. If the goodness of God is a reason you struggle to relate to God freely and without feeling awkward because of feelings of mistrust, disappointment, or anger, it is important to face how you feel. Begin to dialogue with God or with a trusted, mature friend, or with a counselor. Press past the awkwardness and share honestly about your struggles. God already sees your struggles and He is ready and willing to help you work through it!

Being Afraid of God

Some of us may be more afraid of God than we realize because of inaccurate views we've carried about Him that stem from experiences during our upbringing. The following Bible passage describes Jesus as He appears in heaven:

The hair on his head was white like wool, as white as snow, and his eyes were like blazing fire. His feet were like bronze glowing in a furnace, and his voice was like the sound of rushing waters. In his right hand he held seven stars, and coming out of his mouth was a sharp, double-edged sword. His face was like the sun shining in all its brilliance. (Revelation 1:14-16 NIV)

What is your first reaction to reading this passage? Joy? Fear? Intimidation? Does reading this passage draw you closer to Jesus? Or do you feel farther away from Him and more like a servant who needs to bow before a feared King? Most likely, your reaction to this passage correlates to how you see God in your relationship with Him and how you come before Him in prayer.

God's love is so deep it can cause you to question the way you're living, but it's also a love that draws you into your destiny and opens up dreams. It's the love of a Father who brings identity and safety. Do you feel safe in His love? Take time to process that question for a moment.

If you feel any awkwardness in your times with God, I urge you to sit in the awkwardness with Him, rather than shutting down and moving away. Begin to ask God questions that will cause you to confront the things that make you feel awkward in your silence with Him. Here are some practical questions you can use to open the dialogue:

- God, why does this feel awkward right now?
- What do you want to do in me that I'm trying to avoid?
- Why can't I sit still with you?
- What in my belief system and in my heart do I need to change?

I urge you to try this, regardless of whether you hear a response, keeping in mind that the answers to your questions may come later. The goal of time with God is relationship and dialogue, not always an answer. Remember, God is patient. He can wait for years—but it doesn't have to be that long, if we press in for more!

I love the story Jesus tells of the persistent widow, which teaches us to never quit praying:

> *Then Jesus told his disciples a parable to show them that they should always pray and not give up. He said: "In a certain town there was a judge who neither feared God nor cared what people thought. And there was a widow in that town who kept coming to him with the plea, 'Grant me justice against my adversary.' For some time he refused. But finally he said to himself, 'Even though I don't fear God or care what people think, yet because this widow keeps bothering me, I will see that she gets justice, so that she won't eventually come and attack me!'" And the*

*Lord said, "Listen to what the unjust judge says. **And will not God bring about justice for his chosen ones, who cry out to him day and night? Will he keep putting them off? I tell you, he will see that they get justice, and quickly.** However, when the Son of Man comes, will he find faith on the earth?" (Luke 18:1-8, emphasis mine, NIV)*

The gold in this passage is that Jesus is saying, "Bug Me; don't leave Me alone; cry out to Me day and night. Be annoying, be persistent, pull on Me until you get an answer."

Jesus says He can handle it.

He *wants* to be bothered, so bother Him with your prayers. Feel free to share your need, your thoughts, and your questions. He is big enough and He can handle everything you share.

Dec 19, 2022

Pray this prayer:

Jesus, I want to see You as You truly are. I want to know You like I know a friend. If there's any awkwardness in our relationship, I pray You will bring those areas to my attention, so that I can work through them—and lead me to complete wholeness.

Activation #1:

Close your eyes and picture Jesus standing in front of you. Pay attention to what you feel, hear, and see. Write down what happens. This will help you connect with heaven better as you practice this exercise. Don't be afraid. Jesus will always speak life and encouragement to you.

Activation #2:

When I read the passage in Revelation 1:14-16 that describes the purity of Jesus in heaven, I see intimacy. When I come before Jesus, His purifying nature purifies me and brings me His identity. In thinking about this scripture, I can't help but hear the words and melody to Peter Gabriel's song, *In Your Eyes*. The lyrics in the chorus use some of the same imagery that is written in the above scripture passage; specific phrases like, "The resolution of all the fruitless searches," and, "I see the light and the heat," and "I am complete in your eyes." Whenever I hear that song, I always sing it to Jesus because I know His eyes of flaming fire are flames of love for us! Find Peter Gabriel's song, *In Your Eyes,* online. Listen to it, and as you do, picture Jesus.

Takeaway:

God is not a God of fear. He is the God of love. God is a

good Father who doesn't want His kids living below their potential. Press through any awkwardness with God and bother heaven. Bother heaven with your prayers. Share your heart and give God room to respond. Watch what happens.

CHAPTER 4
SILENCING BUSYNESS

"Without great solitude, no serious work is possible."
[1] – Pablo Picasso

When I was a child my dad was always working on our house, making improvements or fixing something. My mom was cooking, on the phone, cleaning, or ironing. Add to the activities of my parents a television set in our living room that was often turned on, three busy siblings, and a grandmother who lived with us, and it all made for a bustling *Big Fat Greek* household where something was always happening.

I found myself wanting to retreat outside to a quiet place. We lived on a hill, so I would climb down its slope and sit on the hidden side of a storage shed my father had built under the trees. I wanted to think in the peace and quiet offered by the absence of television, away from all the noise and activity. As a kid I never mentally processed why I would go down to that spot. I just knew I enjoyed it as a tranquil place where I was alone. It was a place where no one could find me; a place where I could think, dream, ponder, and process.

Over the years, I went to this secret place of solitude many times. When I began commuting to college and work, I used the time in my car as a place to find peace and quiet, and as a place to pray. Then life got busier and without realizing it, I started allowing my schedule to dictate my life. I filled my calendar with *events* and *activities*. My life felt more significant because I was doing more *things*. I was leading a youth group, attending college full-time, taking on side painting projects with my dad, coaching soccer, coaching basketball, and trying to have dating relationships. My alone time had dwindled and though I didn't realize it, I was living with stress. With no time to rest and an overly hectic life, my soul was affected. Eventually, I burned out.

How does burnout express itself? You feel off kilter; you don't want to accomplish anything; you want to zone out and not think about tasks at all. Some people experience burnout in even greater measures than I did, which can lead to increased anxiety and a plethora of soul and heart issues.

I had what some might call *leader burnout,* which was described really well in an article I read. According to the article, here are some of the causes of leader burnout:

- Occupational stressors
- Working long hours
- Expected to be available at all times
- Making major decisions that significantly impacts the company
- Feeling Isolated, Insufficient (or no) support system
- No skills in developing discipline, not setting boundaries
- Not asking for help [2]

Because I was determined to "tough it out," I had to learn the hard way that I needed help and I needed rest. I felt important in my busyness and didn't want to show weakness to those around me or be a person who couldn't hold it together. But I didn't have the tools to create times of rest. As a result, I became exceedingly passive in life and in faith. To distract myself, I turned to things like video games, movies, pornography, girlfriend after girlfriend, TV, events and activities, and more. Instead of dealing with the issues at hand, I filled my life with things that would numb me to the larger issue of needing quiet time and rest. Even writing about this, I can once again feel the sense of anxiety I experienced during that season of life. I am so ecstatic that I am now in a healed place of well-being!

One of the greatest distractions impacting our ability to hear God is our busyness. That includes the busyness around us as well as the busyness in our own minds. Foster writes, "In contemporary society our Adversary majors in three things: noise, hurry, and crowds. If he can keep us engaged in 'muchness' and 'manyness,' he will rest satisfied. Psychiatrist Carl Jung once remarked, 'Hurry is not of the Devil; it is the Devil.'" [3]

The Tool of Saying NO

One tool I had to use to help me walk into wholeness and rest was saying "NO" to people. During that time I believed the lie that if I said "no" to my church leaders, I was saying "no" to God. Because I believed this lie, I became the go-to person to get things done. And since I kept saying "yes," my leaders kept asking me to do more. I've since learned from my experience with burnout that it's better to learn saying "no" long before exhaustion causes us to pay the price in physical, mental, and spiritual health. I would rather be respected for my *no* than walked over for my *yes*.

I had a friend who couldn't say "no." He once promised to come and help me with a project at my house. But before arriving on the day and time we'd scheduled, my friend canceled. We rescheduled, and once again he called to cancel. And then it happened again, and again.

Usually, he would call to cancel because he was on another project that wasn't quite finished, and he needed more time. But each time he was scheduled to come to my home, I had rearranged my work schedule to be home for his arrival. So after he canceled for the umpteenth time, I got frustrated. His choice to always say "yes" was negatively affecting my life, to the point that I finally spoke to him about it. When I explained my frustration with him, he shared with me his struggle with saying "no" because he felt he had to please everyone.

We *all* must learn to say "no," but if we haven't learned how to do so earlier in life, it may not be easy for us. When friends ask us to help them, or invite us to do an activity with them, we might say "yes" because turning them down makes us feel like we're uncaring friends. Each of us will be confronted with this essential lesson of learning the courage to say "NO." We live to please God, not man or our schedules. Eventually we'll let people down in life by saying "no," but that's okay. We don't have to fear man or please people. If we live under that pressure, we will never be free to be ourselves.

Saying "yes" to everyone will cause someone to eventually be unhappy with you because you overcommitted and had to back out on them (Matthew 5:37). Or, saying "yes" will fill your schedule and lead you to feel overstressed and anxious. It might even lead to burnout. If that's you: if you feel you are facing any of the symptoms of burnout mentioned earlier, consider talking with a friend, a counselor, or a leader in your life to create a plan on how to overcome and resolve your struggles with busyness. Don't *tough it out* and end up paying the price personally. Try to balance your schedule every week. See if you can cut out some commitments that are non-essential. You NEED time for YOU. No one will carve out that time for you, so you need to be intentional about your schedule. Your time is precious, and as a rule of thumb, most people will respect your "no."

Living In The Light

As already mentioned in chapter one, it is entirely possible that we keep busy because being quiet would mean facing realities we don't want to face. We can easily use work, play, and distractions from morning until evening to keep us from dealing with issues that need our attention.

When I was unknowingly headed toward burnout, online chatting, email, and cell phones were emerging into the world and adding more busyness into my already overloaded life. I'll share a more in-depth discussion on media and its influence in chapter 10, but for now it's enough to express that these technologies kept me distracted. And to a great degree, I used them as a form of escape from the stress of a life that had gotten out of control.

It's no different today. Digital platforms and social media continue to bombard us with the temptations to have more, to be more, and to fill our time and schedules with many distractions. And all of it affects our time with God. Author Richard Foster writes in *Celebration of Discipline*, that we as humans would rather have someone else talk to God for us: "We are content to have the message second-hand" and not go to God directly, which "saves us from the need to change, for to be in the presence of God is to change." [4]

It's true, God's presence can seem like the light I recently installed in my garage. The previous bulb above my workspace had been too dim for the projects I was doing, so I replaced it with a really bright LED light. A few hours later I walked into the garage to get something and turned on the newly installed light. The new LED startled me because it was so brilliant in comparison to the previous light!

For some of us, coming to God is like that. We can freak out because of His brightness, which illuminates everything it touches. His light can seem almost glaring as it reveals the thoughts in our hearts, especially if we come before Him feeling ashamed, unclean, or dirty. So we keep ourselves distracted. We stay busy with other pursuits and avoid the bright light of God's presence.

I had to face the fact that my own busyness was to avoid facing issues in my life. Willingly letting the brilliant light of God shine in my life has changed me. Where I once lived in fear, I now experience love. Where I once felt afraid of God, I now enjoy intimate friendship. The payoff of letting the light reveal my issues has given me the power to silence busyness and exchange it for peace.

Living From Quietness in a Busy World

Wouldn't it be incredible if your life was like Abraham's, where daily life was lived in a quiet desert, with little to distract? Wouldn't you think that's an ideal place to live to hear God better? Wouldn't it be wonderful to pack up and go find a place where you could live in that kind of quiet solitude?

It's a great idea, but for many, apart from setting into our schedules intentional times to be alone with God, a life of complete solitude in our modern world isn't practical.

For some of us, present circumstances don't allow the possibility of much alone time because of family commitments or financial burdens. So greatly simplifying our busy schedules isn't possible, at least not in the present season.

Yet here's the good news: We don't have to go to a desert and become a hermit. We can learn to make space for silence and quietness in the middle of our busy lives. Though the last few chapters have encouraged the idea of creating space for quietness, it's important to realize that quiet space isn't always a physical space. *Quietness and stillness are not a place: they are a mindset.* They are qualities we must train ourselves to live in, no matter where we are. We don't need to wait for a quiet place; we can bring the quiet to us!

If we turn our ear to God in the midst of life and allow Him in, He will speak ALL THE TIME. If we're intentional about *listening* and *hearing* throughout our days and weeks, we'll find that place of connection wherever we are, and in every circumstance.

There were plenty of ancient mystics who made vows of silence while they lived, worked, ate and worshiped together with other people in larger communities. For some, their vows of silence lasted for years. It would be fascinating to hear what they learned from their experiences. When they finally broke their silence, I'm sure what they had to say was almost certainly profound and convicting.

I watched a *TED Talk* with a man named John Francis, who spent seventeen years in silence within the context of life's activities. He explained his reason for choosing to be silent and how that decision came to pass. He'd recognized in himself a pattern of wanting to state his opinions to people without actively listening to them. Upset by what he saw in himself, he decided to be silent for one day. He was so affected by that first day, he did it for a second day. In two days he realized how much he could learn from life by *listening* to people, so he made a promise to himself to remain silent for a year. Twenty-seven years old at the time, he decided on his next birthday to reassess what he had learned and choose whether he would begin talking again. His silence lasted seventeen years! And the only reason he broke his silence after so long was because he knew it was time to communicate his story and share with the world what he had gained during that time. [5]

John Francis lived a life of silence while still interacting with others around him. The point for us is to learn how to engage in silence in the midst of life's busyness. The majority of us will never take a vow of silence, but we can learn to take time during the chaos around us to quiet our hearts and minds and focus on God's love and goodness.

You're the only one who knows the source of your busyness, and what is needed in order to find God's presence in your life. Take what you've read in this chapter and present what was highlighted in your heart to God in prayer. He will show you how to meet Him in the context of daily life, and reveal any changes needed to silence busyness.

Pray this prayer: *Dec 21, 2022*

Jesus, break through my busy schedule and meet me where I am. I'm sorry for times when I haven't made you the priority in my life. You are worth it, Lord. You are worth my time and my affection. I pour out my love on you right now, right here. I say that I need you more than I realize. Convict me of things that don't please your heart and lead me in your everlasting ways. You are good and faithful. I love you, Jesus. Amen.

Activation #1:

Examine what your time is filled with and ask the Lord if there is anything you need to add or remove from your life. For example, He might ask you to spend less time with a certain person, or less time on your phone and more time reading and resting. Follow the promptings He puts on your heart.

Activation #2:

Try practicing connection with God throughout your workday. In order to do so, you don't need to stop working. Have a conversation while you work, your spirit with His Spirit, heart-to-heart, praying in your mind, or praying out loud if you're able to do so. Take a break from being mentally or physically busy, to connect in the moment.

Takeaway:

To experience rest, you may need to make some changes in your life. You may need to say "no" to people and activities. Come into the light of God's presence and allow Him to reveal any changes in your time usage that need to happen. The goal is to learn to live in the quiet rest of relationship with God, even in the middle of a full life.

CHAPTER 5
SILENCE AND INNER STRESS

"All men's miseries derive from not being able to sit in a quiet room alone." [1] *– Blaise Pascal*

The same light of God that reveals motives for our busyness also reveals sources of stress in our lives. It touches and lights up everything (John 8:12), but it is not to shame us. Rather, it's to draw us closer to Him in intimacy. He illuminates those things in us that need to be cleansed and offers us an invitation to face them so that relationship can flow once again. He is good (Nahum 1:7). Despite whatever we're feeling, He is good. His goodness doesn't change (Malachi 3:6). We change to become more like Him (2 Corinthians 3:18). We are children of the light, and we come into the light so the light will consume us and remove any areas that do not have light (1 Thessalonians 5:5). We come into the light so His light and love can flow in us and through us.

Facing Inner Stress

Generally speaking, we tend to respond to stressors exactly as our family responded to them while we were growing up. If we haven't been shown healthy ways to deal with the stress in our lives, we'll revert to unhealthy patterns and behaviors that are familiar to us.

John Eldredge says, "If you don't have God, and have him deeply, your soul will go in silent search of other lovers."[2] You may have watched a parent or sibling turn to a sedative, prescription drug, alcohol, or to other addictive behaviors. It is possible you've repeated the cycle because you were never shown a healthier choice for what to do when life gets tough. Even as you read this, you may be thinking about what you turn to during stressful times.

As teenager I watched some people in my life deal with stress by retreating and hiding, pretending it would go away, and completely ignoring the problem at hand. I learned from them and did the same in my own life. As I mentioned in the previous chapter, I chose activities like video games, watching movies, going to events, and being with girlfriends to deal with stressors in my life. I now know hiding is not a suitable form of stress relief. It *is* numbing, but it doesn't deal with pain.

To avoid facing an issue I often watched a movie or a TV series. Being entertained kept my mind off the situation or problem, until I became so tired I fell asleep and no longer had to deal with it—at least not immediately. One book title has stated about current culture, that we are "Amusing Ourselves to Death."[3] That was me. And I'd been doing it for most of my life.

But who are we kidding? That issue is not going away. It will surface in our dreams. It'll chase us down with a vengeance and haunt us. And then, because of avoidance, we discover it's no longer a minor issue, but over time it's grown into an enormous monster we're afraid of confronting. Fear makes it seem larger than life. As a result, we have to figure out a way to not only numb the stressor, but also numb the fear.

When I first read the Eldredge quote above, I was single, living alone in an apartment, and dealing with massive feelings of loneliness. During that time I went through a painful two-year process of facing the truth about my inner misery. Whenever I wanted to deal with a personally difficult stressor, my go-to response was to call a friend or a family member and work it out with them over the phone.

But then God spoke to me and called me to *come to Him before turning to others.* He wanted me to talk with Him about my needs. Once I remember attempting to call a friend to talk through something on my heart. My friend didn't answer his phone and I said in my mind, *Dang it, I'm going to have to talk to God about this now, and that's not what I want to do.* Often, I would start to call someone and sense God saying to me, *Don't call them to deal with this thing on your heart.* When I say I sensed Him, I mean, I had this *knowing* in my heart that He was not about to let me prostitute my heart out to others to receive the affection He wanted to give me. Deep in my soul, God was breaking off of me the fact that I was looking to others for my sense of self-worth and value.

I hated many moments during that season, but God did not want my old ways of handling stress to survive into my future journey with Him. He wanted to be the first love in my heart so I wouldn't keep getting disappointed and hurt from putting the love of other things or relationships in that place in my heart only He could fill. He wanted to be everything to me.

That season was a time of being retrained by God to face life and not hide, and to make my friendship with Him my life priority. Since then, life stresses haven't entirely disappeared. But I am learning how to wield this sword called *Silence* to calm myself down and find my true peace in prayer.

This passage in The Passion Translation speaks about God's faithfulness to rescue us when we come and wait in stillness:

> *I am standing in absolute stillness, silent before the one I love,* **waiting as long as it takes** *for Him to rescue me. Only God is my Savior, and He will not fail me.*

(Psalm 62:5, TPT, emphasis mine)

So many of our internal and external stressors can be dealt with or healed through this one step of choosing to stand in quietness before God, waiting as long as it takes for His rescue. He wants to be our first choice for a confidant. He is our ultimate Savior for every course correction we might need to make and every personal need we may have.

The reason I crashed emotionally during the burnout I wrote about in chapter four was because I'd kept all my hurt and pain bottled up inside. God knew it all needed to come out in order for my healing to occur. After walking with God through that season of learning to be vulnerable with Him and with others, I've now gained high value for relational vulnerability. I've discovered vulnerability helps to heal.

King David and King Saul

King David in the Bible is a great example of a person who was vulnerable in his relationship with God. God called him "a man after my own heart," because David laid bare his heart and soul before God (1 Samuel 13:14). He didn't run *from* God when he struggled. He ran *to* God. That's what God longs for: passionate people who bare their souls to Him with openness and transparency. He is after true and intimate connection with humans.

We can learn from the stories of King Saul and King David, to respond to the light of God, and to the correction of God and others, with a teachable spirit and without defensiveness or denial. Neither King was perfect. In fact, both kings sinned grievously. David was a murderer and an adulterer and Saul struggled with jealousy, anger, and more. But in terms of their choices to run **to** God, only one king chose well.

King Saul had experienced God. He'd prophesied and been touched by the Spirit of God. But he showed no vulnerability with God or with people. Unlike King David, Saul did not have a teachable spirit. Most importantly, he never learned to *wait* on God.

When the prophet Nathan confronted David about his sin with Bathsheba, David confessed his sin and truly repented. As for Saul, when God sent the prophet Samuel to speak correction to him, he did not respond well or take responsibility, but made excuses and blamed others. In effect, Saul wanted the blessings of God but neglected to build a relationship with Him (2 Samuel 12).

If you are living in a way you know is not pleasing to God, don't deny it, as Saul did. Instead, go into the secret place with God. Dig in and ask Him, "Why am I doing this? Why am I turning to other things rather than to you? Why can I not surrender this area of my life to you?" There is often something under the surface that these questions will reveal, something tucked away in your life experience that carries hurt, pain, or confusion, or possibly an area in your heart you have not yet yielded to God. He will not reject you if you come to Him with sin. God is *for you* and desires to bring you into freedom from all bondage that hinders you or affects your relationship with Him. God doesn't want you to carry the inner stress of sin or bondage. He wants you to live in peace as His child!

Author Henri Nouwen, in his book *The Way of the Heart,* writes about solitude being a place where God purifies us and transforms us. In his words, it is "the place of *the great struggle* and *the great encounter."* It is a struggle because Jesus is changing us to appear more like Him. It is an encounter because salvation is found in solitude: as Nouwen writes, it is "the place where Christ remodels us in his own image and frees us from the victimizing compulsions of the world." [4]

Failure Doesn't Exclude Us

Like King David and King Saul, we will fail. It's part of the human condition. King David was a great example for us of what to do when we fail God through our sinful responses. He brought all his *mess* to God and received cleansing in his heart. As a tremendous example of David's dialogues with God about his sin, take time to read Psalm 51.

In the New Testament we find the story of the prodigal son, perhaps one of the most beloved parables of Jesus, revealing the heart of God as He responds to sinful failures. In the middle of his deep failure as a son, the prodigal came to his senses and declared to himself, "I will go home and work as one of my father's hired servants." Clearly, he felt ashamed and undeserving of his former place as a son. But if the story had ended with the prodigal son working as a servant and having to pay his father back for all the inheritance money he'd spent, grace and mercy would be irrelevant! Instead, the father of the prodigal reinstated his long-awaited son to full son ship, giving him His own signet ring and celebrating his return with an enormous party.

When we fail God through sinful responses, it can cause us to believe we can't approach Him. It can cause us to carry shame in our lives. In turn, we can view our own hearts as abominable, or as evil. Whatever the negative rhetoric is, if we embrace it, we then come to believe it in our minds. And it causes us to decide we're unable to connect with God, or that we're unworthy to connect with God. And then, like the prodigal son, we can fall into a trap of thinking we have to *work* to prove ourselves to God. The prodigal was resigned to being demoted from his position as a son, to working as a hired hand on his father's farm. He'd even prepared a speech to give to his dad about his own unworthiness.

But that is not how the Kingdom of God operates. Hebrews 4:16 tells us, "Let us approach the throne of grace with **confidence**." No matter how we feel or what we are dealing with, God has instructed us to come to Him *confidently*. What an empowering scripture! We're not to approach the throne of God with our heads hanging down in fear or sadness. We are to come with humility and a repentant heart, but in confidence, knowing He will meet us as the prodigal father lovingly met his wayward son.

Countless times while in corporate worship, I have experienced what I can only describe as the presence of God. I would be worshiping with my head down, feel God's presence in the room, and sense that I needed to stop looking down and instead, look up to heaven. The first time it happened a thought and feeling accompanied it and came to my heart in the form of a question: "Why are you worshiping me with your head down? You are worthy. I have made you worthy! Look up to heaven! That is where your gaze belongs; that is where it needs to be set."

Over a period of several years, whenever I felt the presence of God in corporate worship, it was as if I also felt someone pulling my chin to look up. I recognized that God was breaking me of feeling unworthy in my approach to Him and reminding me of my son ship. He was removing my sense of approaching Him as a judge in His courtroom. Instead, God was showing me He'd made me worthy to come to Him as a son and a friend. He was correcting my self-perceptions to align them with His truth.

As David says in Psalm 3:3 (ESV), "But you, O Lord, are a shield about me, my glory, and the **lifter of my head.**"

There are times in worship when I am completely wrecked and in awe of the presence of God, and I'm on my face, prostrate on the ground. At other times I feel led to kneel before Him with my head bowed. I imagine many of us have had these types of awestruck experiences in God's presence. But as God's sons and daughters we must know, that even in those moments of humility, reverence, and honor, we come with complete access to Him, with freedom to approach Him in confidence and assurance.

Circumstantial Failure

Thus far we've looked at failures that happen as a result of sin. But some failure occurs as part of our journeys in life, as part of the circumstances of our human growth and discovery. There is a wonderful modern-day story about persevering through circumstantial failure, told through the movie, *The Matrix*. Neo, the protagonist, failed his first jump in the *simulation practice arena*. If he'd stopped trying after his first jump, the movie's momentum would've died in the face of a moping antihero. But in his failure, Neo had the encouragement of his entire team and his leader Morpheus. They believed he could do greater things. So Neo didn't give up. He tried again. And as Morpheus had envisioned, Neo went on to do great things.

Another real-life modern-day example of dealing with failure is told by Denzel Washington. During a powerful commencement speech he made the following statement: "If you fall, make sure you are falling forward and not backward." Denzel went on to share about his own early audition failures as an actor and his determination to pick himself up afterward. Thirty years later, his refusal to quit won him a Tony for his role in a play that was performed in the very theater where he'd first failed at an audition.

Come to the Father Openly

Nothing should keep us from coming to God; no failure, no inner stressor, and no awkwardness. If we desire intimacy with God, we'll need to understand that obedience, vulnerability, and an open heart are important to our Father. And now that I am a father, I understand why. As good fathers, we want our children to come to us with open and vulnerable hearts, and with trusting natures that are safe in obedience. Our Father also wants us to come to Him with the same childlike transparent hearts that trust and follow His leadership. He wants us to bring our inner stressors to Him and trust Him to help us find healing.

When I see my kids being themselves (silly, goofy, or hilarious; or when they're hurting, frustrated, or fighting), it pleases me as a father when they approach me freely with whatever is in their hearts. Because they have complete freedom to approach me as their earthly father, when they grow into their relationship with God as their heavenly Father, they will be able to approach Him with complete freedom.

We all battle things in our lives that make us feel we can't approach God freely. But in fact, He wants us to be ourselves as we meet Him. Like David, like the movie character Neo, like Denzel Washington, like the prodigal son, and like so many others, we can pick ourselves up and refuse to quit. If we fail and give up, we won't move forward; we'll move backward. We'll become a victim and feel sorry for ourselves, and that will lead to moping around, sadness, and depressed thinking. In our faith, there is no room for staying in those negative places of our inner stressors!

Pray this prayer:

Lord, help me turn to you when I feel stressed and I can't focus. You have all the answers I need. Give me wisdom to choose what is right in every situation. I recognize that You have enough hope and joy in your arsenal to cover my every moment. May I be like an open book before you, pouring my heart out to you as King David did, because you can handle my stuff. You're big enough! I trust You, and I love You. Amen.

Activation #1:

Are you numbing pain? Sit with God and ask Him to reveal any places where you may be hiding pain or numbing issues of the heart. If you sense there are those places within you, ask Him to show you what to do and how to respond. He is the only One who knows the best pathway for your healing, whether it's through dialogue with Him, or also reaching out for help to others.

Activation #2:

Sit with God as you consider this question: Were you afraid of approaching your parents while growing up because they responded poorly? How has this affected the way you approach God now? Ask God if there are any lies you believe about Him as a result of parental responses. If He shows you a lie, repent, receive His FULL forgiveness, and then ask Him to speak His truth to you, to replace the lie.

Takeaway:

Being vulnerable with God and others who are safe people is incredibly valuable. It can relieve your inner stressors and remove the sting of failure. God doesn't want you to live in stress or stay in failure. Sitting with Him in quiet conversations can lead to living from those places of rest and joy that He has for your life. He is waiting for you in the secret place.

CHAPTER 6

SILENCE AND EXTERNAL STRESSORS

"There are times when solitude is better than society, and silence is wiser than speech."[1] *— Charles Spurgeon*

Job Stressors

A few years ago I was buying paint at a local hardware store. The gentleman mixing my paint looked to be in his fifties. I asked him, "How did you end up working at this store?" My curiosity was piqued because based on the wages the store was paying him, I knew he wouldn't be able to afford living in the area. He explained to me that he'd had a government job in Seattle, where quite a few of his coworkers had died from heart attacks. One by one, the stress of the job was killing off his friends. He then expressed something I'll never forget. He said, "The signs were clear that if I stayed in that job, I would die like my co-workers." About his current job, he added, "The worst I could do here is mix your paint wrong and have to make you a new one. That's a stress I can live with." This man had chosen a life that was going to be better for him in the long run. He'd made financial sacrifices to attain a healthier way of living.

I have friends with highly stressful jobs that require them to be on call 24/7. Some have walked away and pursued different lines of work because of the stress in their jobs and the stress of always being on call. One close friend was so stressed and overworked, his doctor told him he needed to take six months off to recover. During the first three to six weeks of his sabbatical, he slept for ten to twelve hours a day. He'd come incredibly close to a mental and nervous breakdown.

Sometimes changing jobs could be the solution to silencing stress caused by external circumstances. If you live in a constant state of stress because of your occupation, it may be time to see what else is out there jobwise. It's not worth sacrificing your health and wellbeing, and it never hurts to go interview elsewhere.

If you are considering a high-stress job, it's helpful to have your doctor or a naturopath check you out to make sure you're physically fit. And of course, the first priority is to get the heart of God on the matter of your occupation and know it is His assignment for your life. God can call you to challenges, and if He does, He'll show you how to thrive in the middle of them. If you want to leave a job (or for that matter, an area or a region) because it's too difficult or hard, ask God about your desires to leave. Allow Him to reveal what's really going on. You may be called to stay but need additional prayer covering. Or you may need a vacation or a time of sabbatical to get renewed vision. The key is to seek God and get clarity.

Peer pressure

Peer pressure can be another huge stressor in our lives, and it isn't just a teenage phenomenon. We've all experienced the pressure of other people pushing us to do things we wouldn't normally choose to do.

Peer pressure during my college years caused me to make some very unwise choices and almost got me arrested. A friend and I had rented a car and driven from Northern California to visit a friend at a Southern California university. When we arrived at the university, our friend and his roommate jumped in our SUV and began pressuring me to take the car off-roading behind the baseball fields at his school. He explained people had done it before, so I assumed it was permissible and safe and agreed to do it. Unfortunately, a campus security guard on duty had a different understanding than my own. The security guard's vehicle lights turned on, which should've been my cue to stop driving. But one of my college friends kept egging me on, promising that we could get away from the security car, since other people had gotten away before. I followed his lead and things turned into a game of cat-and-mouse between our car and the security guard's car. I darted back and forth, trying to get off the campus without being caught. But apparently, this security guy had been beaten before and wasn't about to let it happen again. I drove back and forth behind the field two or three times trying to lose him. By that time in our little chase, it was dark enough, so I figured if I parked my car in the dead-end lot in the middle of hundreds of other cars, we could get out and sneak away, and return later to pick up the rental car. We bailed, and I waited ten minutes before returning to the parking lot where I'd hidden the car among the sea of other vehicles.

I came back to a rental car with a yellow lock boot on the tire. The security guard was waiting for us. As we approached him, my friend taunted the guard, saying he didn't have the authority to do anything about our situation. That only made the guard more aggravated. I told my friend to stop, and I apologized, explaining the whole situation to the guard. Just then, the police showed up. He'd called the cops! They questioned us, but thankfully, the security guard never pressed charges, so we were free to go. I learned a valuable lesson that day, and it was this: *I could no longer let the voices in my life be louder than the voice of my conscience.*

As a parent, I watch peer pressure impact my young children. As lovely as they are when it's just our family at home, for some reason when their friends come over, a lot of our family rules go out the window. Why? Peer pressure, fun, adrenaline, and excitement take over, and my kids 'choose' to forget our rules for the moment.

How many times have we done the same with God? Have we compromised by giving priority to other voices while setting aside His leading? Each time we give priority to another voice above God's voice, we are minimizing our friendship with our heavenly Father. The cost in intimacy is never worth the momentary price we've paid.

As an adult, I've had to learn how to say NO as part of relieving pressure that comes from others. It has been a process and I haven't always chosen well. But I've come to realize I will always have choices to make concerning my priorities. If I choose well and follow the leading of the Spirit of God, I can stay in the place of peace that God has designed for me to live in as my norm.

Performance And Striving

Another stressor that can deeply affect our lives is our need to perform for God and others. Performance can create all sorts of chaos that prevents us from experiencing rest and peace. The motives for our striving and performance usually come from an internal stressor, but since striving and performance often affect our schedules, our jobs, and our personal lives, I've included the subject in this chapter as an external stressor.

As a young Christian I thought the measure of my intimacy with God was based on how well I performed at work, at church, and in other activities. I had not yet grasped the concept of BEING with God. I was DOING things for His approval because that was the extent of my understanding at the time. But as I came to discover, living the Christian life from a place of performance is frustrating. My striving to perform for God required tremendous energy! My soul was stressed, and my body was tense with the effort of trying to measure up to some invisible standard. And because of my desire to please others, my over-committed schedule was always a personal stressor.

Thankfully, God used circumstances in my life to get my attention and begin moving me out of a performance mindset and into a place of greater rest. In my twenties I owned and operated a painting business. Deciding I needed to secure a down payment on a house and look like a responsible adult, I pushed myself to get more painting jobs and make more money. It just so happened that work was abundant, so even though I was stressed and performing at a level beyond my emotional and mental capacity to focus, I continued to push harder.

One hot, blistering summer day while painting a client's garage, I was rushing to get finished and made a huge mistake that cost me dearly. A piece of metal on the garage door frame tore a horrific gash in the skin around my eye. An initial trip to the ER was followed later by a visit to the plastic surgeon. Unable to work while my eye healed, the accident set my work schedule back by six weeks and cost me thousands of dollars in medical bills.

A week after the accident a friend said to me, "Maybe God is going to use this and teach you something through it." I thought to myself, *What a weird way to learn a lesson, by getting hurt like this!* But a few weeks later, as I sat down to read the well-known and loved Psalm twenty-three, God spoke clearly to me. "The Lord is my Shepherd, I shall not want. He makes me lie down in green pastures..." The words "HE MAKES ME LIE DOWN" jumped off the page and my jaw dropped at the revelation I was receiving. I knew the lesson I needed to learn: I was always in a hurry! God wanted to use this opportunity to slow me down and show me HE is my Provider. He wanted me to lie down in green pastures, meaning, it was never His intention for me to live a life of striving and being driven to perform. His plan was for me to be at rest, even while I worked hard.

I don't believe for a second that God caused my accident, because He's a good Father who only wants what's best for me and for all His children. But He used my mistake (and the ensuing consequences) to teach me His ways. During my down time from the accident I realized I had never understood the concept of rest. Instead, I lived under tremendous fear, worry, and anxiety (Philippians 4:6-7). God needed to remove them from my life and give me a new understanding that would become a better foundation for how to work and live. As Psalm twenty-three had promised, God was leading me by the quiet waters and restoring me gently.

By the time I returned to work I had gained a new mindset about what was most important. The priority was to be at rest with God's plan for my life and to trust He will come through for me. I'd learned that making more money was not worth the cost of giving up my peace and rest. I stopped pushing myself so hard. I began to relax more and stop to enjoy the people, experiences, and environment around me.

A few years ago I asked God, "What's my purpose?" When I asked that question, I was asking for direction about where He wanted me to be serving in the church or in ministry. I heard Him say to my heart, *Your purpose is to be loved.* God-conversations like these are why silence and recalibration are so incredibly important. Clearly, I didn't get the point, so the next day I asked the Lord, "What do you want me to do?" I was asking for direction again about where He wanted me to be serving. He responded to me lovingly, yet emphatically, with *Stop asking me that and seek My face.*

His response made me realize I had approached Him as a Master in order to figure out what He wanted me to *do*. But rather than responding to me as His servant, God had responded to me as His friend. He just wanted me to spend time with Him.

A few months after that prayer I was talking with a friend about an experience he had at a motivational speaker's conference. One assignment they gave him during a particular session was to write down what he felt was his purpose. He wrote down, *To be loved.*

When he shared his purpose with me, I was astonished. God was confirming what I'd heard from Him a few months earlier. My friend and I both understood that by being loved first by God and resting in that, everything else in life would work itself out.

Here is the point: if you want to **do** more things for God, ask Him first. He discerns your capacity and what you can handle. The reality is, He doesn't need us to do anything. He doesn't need our help to get things done. He chooses to partner with us to get things done, but God is concerned about connection, not production.

Other Stressors

We'll never be able to cover the entire list of external stressors in this chapter. But the principle for every stressor of life is that when we feel stress, we go to God for clarity and understanding. We get alone in the secret place and meet Him as a good Father, waiting on Him. We ask, seek, and knock, until we sense His Fatherly wisdom and guidance. If we don't hear an answer immediately, we continue to lay our stressors before God and trust He will answer.

Some stressors may not be immediately evident because of our own mindsets. Stringing along a boyfriend or girlfriend primarily to avoid loneliness, with no plans for marriage; staying in a job because the pay is good, but the environment is toxic; purchasing a vehicle out of desire and being saddled with expensive monthly payments; stressors like these may require heart examination with God to discover what is creating the gut sense of stress and tension.

The reality is, when you finally create space for silence in your life, you'll begin to perceive the areas of your life that are creating stress for you. Practicing silence and waiting before the Lord will quiet the voice of the enemy and also silence other negative voices (including negative self-talk). Times of quiet in God's presence will enable you to begin destroying the negative power of internal and external stress in your life.

Pray this prayer:

Lord, thank you that You care about my life and the stress I experience. I come to you and ask You to lead me into Your presence. Give me Your wisdom and understanding. I choose to yield to Your plans for my life and make changes You reveal to me. Thank you, Jesus. I love you. Amen.

Activation:

Is there an external stressor you might need to adjust in your life in order to live a fuller and healthier life? Take time to pull away and be with God. In that place of quietude, ask Him what He thinks about the situations where you need discernment. As before, ask for His advice and wisdom. Wait for him in stillness and confidence. He will answer in the right time and the right way.

Takeaway:

External Stressors can cause disruption and keep us from experiencing the quiet rest of God. Bringing our lives before God as an open book and inviting Him to reveal sources of stress will help us move toward solutions and bring relief from stress that robs our peace.

CHAPTER 7
FINDING CLARITY

"Silence isn't empty, it's full of answers." – Anonymous

Each morning I wake up and ask God this question: "What are you doing in me today?" I always hear an answer. Some days the answer is the same as the day before, and at other times I am surprised with a new and fresh response. James, the brother of Jesus, wrote in James 4:2-3, "We don't have because we don't ask." I have to say, when I wonder why I'm not hearing God's voice or when heaven seems to be quiet, it's usually directly related to the fact that I'm not checking in with God, and I'm not asking questions. I'm pretty convinced almost everything in heaven starts with a question!

One morning I asked the Lord to show me something new about silence. Here is what I heard in my heart: *Silence is deliberate and intentional* and it is a *determiner in our relationship with the Lord.* It is intentionally seeking Him out, wanting to know more about Him, and to find out what He is doing. James also wrote, "Draw near to God and he will draw near to you" (James 4:8). God is ready to draw near to me, but He asks me to take a step toward Him. It may be a small step, but it only takes a step.

Jesus often made time to be alone in prayer. He either woke up early and intentionally retreated from others, or He purposefully slipped away from ministry demands during the day and sought out a quiet place of prayer (Luke 9:18). His purpose was to connect with the Father. That's why Jesus said in John 5:19, "I only do what I see my Father doing." Through those personal times with His Father in heaven, Jesus saw what God was doing. As a result, He lived His life out of Their communion together.

Silence requires focus. If we'll pull away and focus, we can receive clarity from God. We can process dreams or visions. We can get more clarity as we hash out the details in our thoughts, as we ask questions, and as we seek advice. Deliberate, intentional focus in our times with God will bring the connection and the answers we need. We can choose what to focus on in silence, but without intentionally turning toward God and giving our attention to Him, we may struggle to connect.

Psalms 32:8 says, "I will instruct you and teach you in the way you should go, I will counsel you and watch over you." When I silence my heart to listen, God will speak to me throughout my day. By no means have I mastered the art of hearing God while working, but when I have stopped to listen and tuned my heart to His voice, I have experienced breakthrough moments when He speaks instruction and counsel, or when I speak to Him and ask questions.

Clarity in Decision-Making

One of the wonders of our relationship with God is that He is utterly faithful to guide us and give us clarity in all our decisions. More than once, God has personally saved me, and my family, from making serious mistakes. One such situation occurred in 2006, when I decided it was time to own property. I'd already saved up a decent down payment, and the loans offered at the time were incredible. For the amount of money I was making, it seemed to be an easy decision. I also thought real estate in the area would only continue to increase in value, and I didn't want to miss my opportunity to snag a property that could gain some serious equity. But in all my searching for a home or a condominium to purchase, I only felt an anxiety and lacked internal peace about the process.

I asked the Holy Spirit for His guidance and sought advice from my parents. Mom and Dad felt uneasy about my idea of buying property. I finally realized there was a clear red flag telling me not to buy. Though it wasn't easy, I gave up on the idea.

God cares about our lives and our purchases, because in the end everything is His anyway. Within two years the economy took a nosedive and tanked through a mortgage crisis that fueled a deep and widespread recession. I am so thankful I was asking the Holy Spirit for clarity and that I responded to His voice and to my parents' wisdom. Had I purchased a home, the mortgage crisis would've most likely thrown me into deep financial challenges and debt. Asking questions and intentionally seeking God in the matter kept me from a purchase that would've had dire consequences for my life.

Another time I was struggling with making a decision about whether to buy a used truck. I'd been searching online for weeks for a good deal. I knew in my gut and in my spirit that it would not be the best decision. My wife even supported the purchase, but I could not reconcile the lack of peace in my soul and spirit with my decision to buy a truck, when I already owned one. I took it to a time of prayer. Quieting myself in His presence, I asked God, "Lord, can I buy another truck?" I felt a question come to my heart, *Why do you need a truck? Your truck works fine. Why don't you wait and buy a NEW truck later?*

I trusted God and His wisdom and chose to forego buying a truck. If He was telling me to wait, then it was better to wait. He saw the future opportunities that will come that I wasn't aware of in that moment. His plan was better than mine. And besides, He'd said a NEW truck. That was much better than a USED truck! Everything I owned was His anyway. His direction quieted the questions and brought the clarity I needed.

It's when we dialogue with Him about our life (about major decisions and minor decisions) that we discover He LOVES the dialogue. He LOVES the connection. Nothing thrills His heart more than the fact that we would open a dialogue with Him about the details of our lives! The writer of Hebrews 11:6 has said it well: that God rewards those who diligently seek Him.

Take a moment and ponder these five brief passages about God's leading:

Job 23:10—"He knows the way that I take; when he has tested me, I will come forth as gold" (NIV).

Proverbs 16:3—"Commit to the Lord whatever you do, and your plans will succeed" (NIV).

Proverbs 16:9—"In their hearts humans plan their course, but the Lord establishes their steps" (NIV).

Isaiah 30:21—"Whether you turn to the right or to the left, your ears will hear a voice behind you, saying, 'This is the way; walk in it'" (NIV).

Isaiah 55:12—"You will go out in joy and be led forth in peace…" (NIV).

Do you need clarity in your life and in your decision-making? God already sees the way and He has the answers. I encourage you, lean into Him. Ponder these above passages in your heart and allow them to draw you closer to Him. Let joy, peace, and His voice guide your steps.

Learning to Discern God's Voice

Part of gaining clarity when communicating with God involves learning to discern His voice. Several summers ago I learned an important lesson about discernment. I was renovating our backyard. We had a company build a beautiful swimming pool for us. I then began to build a wooden deck around the pool. Completing the deck was the final project I needed to do before the backyard was finished. When I was two boards away from finishing this five-week project, I heard a voice whisper to me inside my heart, *Now is the time to sell your home.*

I thought it was the devil. Why would the Lord tell me to sell my house right when I got it where I wanted it? Let me also say that when this happened the humidity outside was off the charts, the sun was beating down on me, it was the end of a long day and I felt dehydrated and mentally hazy. So naturally, I thought to myself *I'm delirious. I'm hearing things.*

The next weekend at church a friend came up to me and said, "I just felt I needed to tell you that You don't hear the enemy's voice. You hear the Lord's voice." It was confirmation for me that what I'd heard was the Lord's voice and not my own thoughts or the enemy's voice. In obedience I sold my home, and God began to reveal a new plan for the direction of our family that involved moving to another state.

Don't worry, if God wants to get His point across to you, He will make sure you have everything you need to understand His communications or make the right decision. When you dialogue with God and talk to Him about the things in your life, trust Him. He may answer right away or later in a dream, through a friend, or through a door of opportunity that opens unexpectedly. Keep your heart tender and open. Hold your life with open hands and let Him respond.

Once, I was reading the Bible story of Joshua and the battle of Jericho to my children. During the part of the story where the walls fell, I felt the Lord whisper to my heart, *Did you know I only did Jericho once? Why are you fighting today's battles with yesterday's strategies?*

He had my awestruck attention as I took time to ponder the scope of what He was saying. I studied the biblical stories and noticed that for each battle, there was always a new strategy. Nothing was done in the same way as had been done in previous battles.

In the battles we face today, it's no different. The strategy is often unique for each new challenge we face. If we had a game plan that worked every single time, we would never need heaven's help. Needing a *new* strategy in each battle keeps us leaning on God. It requires that we go to Him for guidance.

I'm so thankful God whispers His guidance and wisdom to us. I wonder what opened up the encounter of His voice in that moment while reading to my children. Was I able to sense God's communication because my heart was quiet and open? Certainly, reading the Bible is one way God desires to encounter us. If our minds and hearts will listen, and if we pay attention to what pops out at us during our reading times, the Lord is ready to speak.

What does this communication process with God look like? In one way, it's like those times when you zone out while driving and then wonder how you got to your destination. That happens because the more you travel a route, the more familiar and comfortable it becomes, making it easy to zone out. Like that familiar driving route, when you talk to God and listen regularly, you're creating a pathway in your life for hearing Him. It's called building a history with Him. Over time, through your consistent connection with God, you learn how He speaks, and you're ready to listen when He does. Your heart has become more attuned, and you recognize His voice.

I know my children's voices because I hear them all the time. I hear the laughing, the crying, the screaming, the tantrums, the whining, and the tender whispers. God loves knowing all about us, just as I know all about my children. And in the same way that I come to God all the time, I am known by Him as a son, and I know Him deeply as my Father.

Unlike the driving example of zoning out, we can't tune out our children because they won't let us! Although I will say, moms have a gift of doing this incredibly well—at least, until they hear the *death scream* because a finger got stuck in a slammed door, thanks to another sibling.

What does God's voice sound like? Well, it doesn't sound like James Earl Jones' voice as Mufasa in *The Lion King* movie! It can sound like your own voice, but much smarter! He can infiltrate your thoughts with better thoughts than you could have created in your own thinking process. God will put ideas into your mind, ideas you could not have created. God mainly uses your senses to communicate to you, so the way you hear God's voice may vary. As you just read, you might hear God speaking in the form of thoughts that come to your mind, or as an inner whisper of His words. He may speak to you in the form of a *gut feeling* about a situation, just as Paul wrote in Romans 9:1, that his *conscience bore witness* with God's

Spirit. All these types of communication are forms of *hearing from God*. Of course, we want to make sure everything we hear through our senses aligns with the Word of God. Personal communications from God will always line up with the Bible's truth.

It might be helpful to understand that God's communications with us aren't always straightforward. Jesus taught truths in parables, in part to gauge the level of the people's spiritual hunger for Him. He spoke in parables and sometimes in mysterious and confusing riddles because He wanted to see if people really *wanted* to engage and pursue. To be honest, God can be quite sneaky in His communications, and I think He likes it that way. He enjoys the struggle, the banter, the negotiations, the wrestling. He hides Himself in the everyday and can stay hidden for lengthy periods of time. God enjoys being searched out like a treasure, as Proverbs 25:2 states: "It is the glory of God to conceal a matter; to search out a matter is the glory of kings." God enjoys being hidden, but even more, He enjoys being found by someone who hungers for connection with Him.

Will you search for God hiding in your everyday circumstances? To do so is to your glory as a royal, kingly son or queenly daughter of God!

Hindrances to Clarity

If you've been attempting to *listen* to God but you feel like you're not *hearing* much, don't give up: there is hope. Read the list below of common hindrances to hearing God. If one is highlighted to your heart as something applying to your life, make note of it.

Common Hindrances to Hearing God:

- We don't think we deserve to hear His voice.
- We are afraid He won't say nice things when He speaks.
- We are content with others hearing God for us. (The Israelites preferred that Moses heard God for them, rather than having God speak directly to them—Exod. 20:19)
- We are narrow-minded in our perception of what we think His voice looks or sounds like (e.g., God speaks through our friends, children, movies, or nature: but not in conversation to us).
- We think we have to *do* something to deserve communion with God (rather than understanding we're always free to be with Him).
- We think we have to go to a specific place to hear Him.
- We can't discern between our voice and His voice.
- We don't read the Word very often, so when He

speaks, we have no basis for discerning whether what we're hearing is accurate or inaccurate.
- We have forgotten how to listen.
- We are talking too much.
- We would prefer a quick answer so we can get back to our lives, rather than sitting before Him for the sake of connection.
- We aren't at peace when we are listening (e.g., we're stressed, anxious, fearful, etc.)
- We believe a lie about ourselves or about God.

Are you aware of any hindrances in the above list that stand out to you as affecting your own relationship with God? Tell God you're aware of those hindrances. Ask for His help and wisdom to overcome them (James 1:5). You may need the help of another, more mature believer (or even a counselor) to recognize and deal with stronger blockages. If that is the case, ask God to guide you in the right pathway for pursuing help (Isaiah 30:21). He will help and guide you! Be persistent in taking steps to overcome the hindrances. Your relationship with God is worth the effort.

Believing Lies About God

One hindrance mentioned above has to do with lies we may believe concerning His nature or our own nature.

God has graciously shown me lies that have hindered my ability to know Him and receive from Him. One lie was revealed while serving as part of a ministry team for a weekend event at a small church. The speaker for the evening instructed everyone in the congregation to turn to the person sitting next to them and "Tell them one truth you believe about God." I turned to the one sitting beside me and said something like, "God is faithful." The speaker soon added another instruction: "Now tell that same person one lie you believe about God." After my initial surprise about the instruction we were being given, as clear as daylight, a lie popped into my mind. I turned to the person next to me and said, "I believe the lie that God is holding out on me and He's not giving me His best; that I'm getting the scraps that fall off His table." I bowed my head in that moment and repented to the Lord for believing that lie. I then asked Him to help me trust Him.

Even now I cry at having believed that lie about God. But He is gracious! Believing God was holding out on me was connected to my *fear of missing out*. While growing up I felt like I was missing out on so many things. I felt left out when I wasn't invited to a friend's party or to a particular event that everyone else had been invited to attend. I felt left out when I couldn't go somewhere others were going. I was afraid of missing out on opportunities. It's the reason that as a young adult, I was glued to my cell phone: I didn't want to miss a text that was an invitation to go somewhere. My fear of missing out (FOMO) strengthened my belief in the lie that I was getting second best, both from others and from God.

Lies can keep our hearts from trusting God has our best interest at heart. They can block our hearts from fully being vulnerable and can undermine our intimacy with God. And they can hinder our ability to hear His voice.

To engage honestly and deeply with the Father, begin asking a difficult question: "What lies do I believe about You, God?" Let yourself sit with this question as you come to God. Nothing may immediately come to the surface. But if a lie does come to mind, repent of believing it and ask God to restore you to Him. Ask Him to reveal the TRUTH to counteract the lie. He will do it because He loves you deeply!

Other Hindrances

Some of these final hindrances to clarity may seem a bit odd, but having personally experienced each of them, I wanted to share them to help those who may sense a hindrance but not understand its source. It could be that one of these hindrances applies.

Not Getting Enough Sun

When I was living in California and had enough sun to carry me through the winters, I thought the idea of depression due to a lack of sun was absurd. And then I lived through my first Seattle winter, where most days are mainly gray. I realized why the coffee culture is so thriving there; the caffeine keeps people wired and peppy enough to make it through the dismal winter season!

There is a real physical deficiency called S.A.D., or Seasonal Affect Disorder. When I first experienced the vitamin D deficiency associated with S.A.D., I wasn't sure how I could bring it into my belief system and theology. I'd always been a rather cheerful person, joyful and full of life. But in Seattle I felt unusually depressed and wanted to sleep more than normal. To survive through those winters, I read that some people use a "happy light" that released ultraviolet light similar to the sun's UV rays. Thirty minutes per day under this light was supposed to give relief from symptoms.

Having experienced S.A.D. firsthand, I no longer judge others for experiencing it. During my time in Seattle, I took large doses of Vitamin D and learned to plan a week-long vacation to a sunny destination in the middle of winter. Having suffered from a vitamin D deficiency, I'll share here eight symptoms that could indicate a lack of adequate Vitamin D:

- Often getting sick or infected
- Fatigue and tiredness
- Bone and back pain
- Depression
- Impaired wound healing
- Bone loss
- Hair loss
- Muscle pain [1]

Spiritual Atmospheres

Another reason for vacations or getting away from time to time ties into the benefit of *changing spiritual atmospheres* in order to get clarity. A number of years ago I was working on a remodeling project in my basement. While I was working I was also praying for clarity about a certain situation. But for the life of me, I couldn't receive an answer from heaven. At one point I finally stopped working, walked outside, and knelt down on the grass in my backyard to pray. The answer I was looking for came to me within moments.

I'd spent about four or five days praying about this situation, to no avail. But without realizing it, working indoors for so many hours had created in me a sense of feeling trapped. When I changed atmospheres, something shifted.

Jesus had to remove Himself from certain situations

in order to connect with His Father. You may need to do the same. If you're feeling out of sorts and need to reconnect with God, it may be helpful to discover *where* you feel most clear: on top of a mountain, while driving, while sitting in a certain room or space, while listening to music, or wherever else you sense an open interaction. Find that place or space where you're able to reconnect. You may experience much more clarity in the right physical location for you.

If you live in a place or city where the atmosphere is dark spiritually, you're not alone. For your own sake, you may need to find a place to get away to once in a while—out from under that atmosphere—in order to find refreshment and solace. But God is also more than willing to show up for you in those places where you are called to live. Keep the dialogue open with Him and bring your frustrations to the Lord. Not only can He handle them, He can also show you how to thrive where He's placed you!

Not Taking Care of Ourselves

Another hindrance to clarity could be in the way we treat our bodies. If we're not taking care of ourselves physically, if we're not eating healthily or getting enough sleep, it will be difficult for us to find clarity in life. My wife sometimes reminds me, "You've been eating things with a lot of sugar, and you're not drinking enough water." She's knows me well! And all the while I've been drinking a lot of coffee, which if taken in excessive amounts, actually makes me more nervous.

If we're not treating our bodies well, our bodies will constantly be playing *catch-up*, and we'll lack the mental acuity and physical energy to focus. There is a reason God instituted six days of work followed by one day of rest. He recognizes we need to rest and care for ourselves spiritually, emotionally, and physically. Clarity—spiritual, mental, and even emotional clarity—will be hindered if we're not taking care of our bodies and souls.

Pray this prayer:

Jesus, break things off of my life that are keeping me from hearing you clearly. I ask for vision for my life and clarity about what I need to be doing to fulfill your purposes in me. I ask for fresh ideas on how to keep my relationship with you meaningful, exciting, and full of passion. I never want to just go through the motions with you, Jesus. Encounter me as you have encountered others on their journeys. Speak to me like a friend. I want a deeper relationship with you. I want to long for you like never before. I love you Jesus! Amen.

Activation:

Jesus promises in Matthew 7:7, if you *ask,* God will give; if you *seek,* you'll find; and if you *knock* on the door (of inquiry), you'll discover the door will open. Ask yourself the following questions or process them in times with God. Spend time with each question, allowing it to take you deeper and reveal new possibilities and strategies for a more fruitful and fulfilling life.

- What are the places and/or moments where I connect best with God and can hear Him most clearly?
- What am I daring and willing to ask God about in my life in this season?
- How has my ability to draw near to Him been recently?
- Have I consulted Him in all my decision-making?

Takeaway:

Pulling away to be with God was an essential part of Jesus' earthly life and daily walk. Like Jesus, we need regular, focused, and intentional times with God in order to grasp identity, purpose, and direction. As we ask, seek, and knock, we'll get clarity. And caring for our bodies and souls will keep us rested and healthy so we can get the clarity we need.

CHAPTER 8
BEING AT REST

"Silence and solitude, the soul's best friends." [1] – Henry Wadsworth Longfellow

Rest is physical. Rest is also spiritual. **Physical rest** is essential, not at all secondary in importance. It does so much more than we know in terms of restoring our souls, bodies, and spirits. **Spiritual rest** is also essential and enables us to trust God, even in the middle of difficult circumstances.

Sleep and Rest

As a kid, I remember my father waking up at six o'clock in the morning and heading out the door by seven o'clock. He worked as the supervisor of a mid-sized painting crew for an individual who owned many rental properties in San Francisco.

Dad would always come home from work at the end of his eight-hour workday and take a nap. He grew up in Greece so an afternoon siesta was normal for him. After an hour or two of napping, he woke up and started working on his own projects around home.

Naturally, I thought Dad's daily nap was a normal part of life, so whenever I could, I started taking naps. I've come to love naps! Naps are a happy place for me. When people ask me if I want to join them in lots of activities, I often say, "Let me get a nap in, and then I'll join you later."

Some days I can wake up with my soul feeling off kilter. If I can take a ten to twenty-minute nap later that day, for the most part I will wake up from my nap feeling clear again. It's almost as if a nap gives me a reset that is similar to the reset that happens during a night of sleep.

In fact, studies have shown that a short fifteen to thirty-minute nap can make you more alert, reduce stress, improve cognitive functioning, create added patience, increase reaction time, improve learning, give more efficiency, and foster better health. This study also shows that taking a brief nap eight hours after you wake up is more effective than adding an extra fifteen to thirty minutes to the end of a night of sleep. [2]

In Job 33:15-18, NLT, the writer says of God, "(He) speaks in dreams, in visions of the night, when deep sleep falls on people, as they lie in their beds. He whispers in their ears, and terrifies them with warnings. He makes them turn from doing wrong; He keeps them from pride. He protects them from the grave, from crossing over the river of death."

Some of the details of Job's statement are sobering. But the point of the scripture is that God *speaks* during our sleep. Not only is sleep a time when our physical bodies are recharged, sleep is also a time when God ministers to our *spirit* and *soul* through dreams and visions of hope and direction, and as this passage also reveals, through dreams of warning.

In today's fast-paced culture we often forego getting enough sleep because of the demands of life. But sleep is a way to honor our bodies. Sleep is valuable as a part of living a long and healthy life. We would do well to realize that over our lifetime, getting enough sleep each night helps our bodies heal and stay healthy. And getting enough sleep also helps us to be more positive emotionally because we're not fighting fatigue and the negativity that often comes with it. On a daily basis, sleep helps to reset us in spirit, soul, and body. Sleep isn't just a tag-on to the rest of our lives. Sleep is a valuable aspect of our lives that shouldn't be deemed as unimportant or unnecessary.

Staying at Rest in the Storm

There is another kind of rest that is spiritual, and if we're able to tap into that spiritual rest as a normal way of life, we will weather the storms that come our way. In the Bible there is a well-known story about a nap that Jesus took in a boat in the middle of a storm. The point of the story isn't focused mainly on physical rest, as we've been discussing so far in this chapter. It is about *spiritual rest in turmoil*, the focus of the next section in this chapter:

> *But Jesus was calmly sleeping in the stern, resting on a cushion. So they shook him awake, saying, "Teacher, don't you even care that we are all about to die!" Fully awake, he rebuked the storm and shouted to the sea, "Hush! Calm down!" All at once the wind stopped howling and the water became perfectly calm. Then he turned to his disciples and said to them, 'Why are you so afraid? Haven't you learned to trust yet?"* Mark 4:38-40 (TPT)

The disciples were frantic and frightened, but Jesus was not: He was calm! He was so calm, He slept right through the howling wind and the turbulent waves.

Imagine if we could sleep right through our crazy circumstances and stay at rest! How did Jesus manage to be so at peace? A scripture from Isaiah 26:3 (NKJV) gives us a clue: "You will keep him in perfect peace, *whose mind is stayed on You*, because he trusts in You." The key to keeping ourselves at perfect peace is keeping our mind on God. By inference, if we are keeping our minds on God it means we trust Him. To the extent that we trust God, we will experience peace.

Another way the Scriptures express staying calm in the middle of a storm is with the phrase, "**Be still.**" How many times have we seen that phrase written on plaques, or heard it sung in songs? As a young man moving into the decade of my twenties, I didn't fully understand why people would tell me to *be still*. It was a foreign concept to me, especially if it meant sitting still in class, in a meeting, or at church!

As a biblical concept, "Be still" comes from the passage in Psalm 46:10. In the context of the entire psalm, the phrase clearly defines being still in the midst of difficulties. Look at the words used in this passage to describe what is happening all around the psalmist: *trouble, mountains falling, quaking, kingdoms falling, nations in uproar, the earth melting*. In the middle of the chaotic turbulence the writer uses phrases like, *Be still; we will not fear; God is within her; God will help; the Lord Almighty is with us;* and *God is our fortress*. These phrases speak to the kind of calm Jesus experienced in the boat, fast asleep, while everyone else was in turmoil because of the storm.

Take a moment and thoughtfully read Psalm 46:

God is our refuge and strength, an ever-present help in trouble.

Therefore we will not fear, though the earth give way and the mountains fall into the heart of the sea, though its waters roar and foam and the mountains quake with their surging.

There is a river whose streams make glad the city of God, the holy place where the Most High dwells.

God is within her, she will not fall; God will help her at break of day.

Nations are in uproar, kingdoms fall; he lifts his voice, the earth melts.

The Lord Almighty is with us; the God of Jacob is our fortress.

Come and see what the Lord has done, the desolations he has brought on the earth.

He makes wars cease to the ends of the earth.

He breaks the bow and shatters the spear; he burns the shields with fire.

*He says, **"Be still, and know that I am God;** I will be exalted among the nations,*

I will be exalted in the earth."

The Lord Almighty is with us; the God of Jacob is our fortress. (Psalm 46, NIV, emphasis mine)

Don't our situations feel like this sometimes, as though the whole earth is collapsing in on our emotions? It can seem hard to focus on God's goodness and love because we are so focused on the problem. Yet during this whole passage, God says to "Be still." Be still in the storm; be still in the surrounding craziness. It is counterintuitive for us to *be still* when things are whirling and swirling in our lives. But when God instructs us to do the seemingly impossible, He makes it possible.

Sometimes in prayer I ask God if there is a scripture he wants me to read. Whenever I see the reference *Psalm 46:10* in my mind's eye, I understand the Father is saying to me, "Chris, you need to be still in this moment and in this situation."

Much like my passionate Greek parents, who wear their emotions on their sleeves, I experience a lot of emotions. I'll admit my emotions can be strong, especially when I add to that my deep love and affection for coffee and its caffeine. In the past I would get worked up over a situation and in my mind imagine a fake reality (something that wasn't true, except in my thoughts) about that situation. From there, I would make assumptions based on the worst-case scenario. It often took other people talking me down off the unrealistic story-cliffs I'd concocted in my thoughts, to bring me to a place of recognizing my emotions needed some taming.

When life gets hard, we can get emotional. Someone may glare at us the wrong way or cut us off on the road, and we react strongly. When that happens, the last thing I want to do is to *be still*. That's when part of me would rather live by the scripture, "Vengeance is mine" (Romans 12:19). I've been able to learn over the years (often by doing it the wrong way) that quieting myself and leaning into God's love does two things; His love calms those moments of passion, and quiets the exaggerated storyteller creating scenarios in my head.

Dragon Slayer of Negativity

Our exaggerated mental storytellers can lead us to live from a place of fear, worry, or negativity, but God wants us to live from a place of *Be still*. Following the death of my closest childhood friend, I had to learn how to let go of negative thinking and begin living from a good place in my thought life. Before my friend died at age thirty-nine from a heart problem, I'd never before faced such deep, personal pain or experienced a life event that challenged my belief in God's goodness. For the first time in that season, I found my heart asking, *Is God really good?* During the months following my friend's death I wrestled to find the good in my life because of focusing on my loss and the feeling of being abandoned by God. The struggle to find meaning in daily life was so real that my mind was flooded with suicidal thoughts.

One day I was walking through a big box construction store and heard these lyrics playing over the store's speaker system: "Sometimes I feel like giving up, giving up, giving up..." The lyrics of the chorus were sung over and over, until I thought to myself, *Who is choosing these songs? This is ridiculous!* At that moment, I could feel death, darkness, and suicidal thoughts pulling at me in a strange and obviously dark manner.

A week later I was having a conversation with a friend who had gone through a terrible breakup with his girlfriend. As a result, he struggled with suicidal thoughts and had sought the help of a counselor to overcome them. He shared with me the counselor's advice to him: "You need to find the good in your life right now and stop focusing on the bad." It was a simple truth, yet incredibly powerful. I took his counselor's advice to heart for my own life and heard God confirm it during one of our quiet times together. I was praying and this thought came to my heart, "Stop focusing on what I'm NOT doing in your life and focus on what I AM doing in your life."

You might have a situation in life that seems so heavy, it keeps you from focusing on the good. Take a few moments right now and remind yourself of what is *good* in your life, and then give thanks to God for those things, however great or small. Begin practicing this every day. One idea that may be helpful is to start a *joy journal* on your phone or in a paper journal, to document the good things happening each day, until your outlook changes. I had to practice focusing on the good for months in order to make it through my pain and loss. But I made it through—and you can, too!

Author Richard Foster says we will find joy in our lives by filling our lives with things that are *good* and *simple*, and by always *thanking God* for them. He adds that when we keep our mind focused on those things, "We will be so full of those things, that they will tend to swallow our problems." [3]

A few days after hearing that depressing song in the big box store, I sensed God speaking to my heart in prayer. I asked God one morning, "What are you doing in me today?" In response to my question, I saw a phrase in my mind telling me I was a *Dragon Slayer*. Since that description made no sense to me, I continued about my day and forgot about it entirely.

That night, the Lord spoke to me in an unusual way through my son, who was only three years old at the time. I was sitting in our family room with my wife Katie and our daughter Sophia and son Josiah. Katie and I were cuddling with the kids in a wonderfully quiet moment of togetherness where no one was talking. Suddenly Josiah started singing, "You take your sword in your hand, and you don't give up, and you kill the dragon until he's dead." Immediately, I perked up and remembered what God had spoken to me at the beginning of the day. At first I wondered if Josiah was singing a song he'd heard in a cartoon, but I soon realized it was a supernatural moment. When I glanced over at him, I saw his face and realized he wasn't daydreaming about a cartoon. He was actually hearing something in his spirit from God. I asked him to sing his spontaneous song again, and then a third time. My three-year-old didn't normally sing random words and melody verbatim, but in that moment he repeated it all perfectly, three times in a row. I knew the heavens were speaking to me.

In the following days, through prayer I came to understand the dragon I was being called to slay was none other than my focus on the negative. In prayer and through my son, God was calling me to be strong in my fight to kill these negative thought patterns and habits. I did so slowly, by choosing to not think about them and by reminding myself of the good things in my life. A few months later I was in the same big box construction store and heard the same hopeless song playing over the store's speaker system. I can happily say I was able to laugh and ignore it and move on with my day!

In Psalm 8:2 the writer says, "You have taught children and infants to tell of your strength, silencing your enemy and all who oppose you." This is exactly what God did when He first spoke to me in solitude and called me a Dragon Slayer. Then He confirmed it through my three-year-old son's prophetic song about dragons. Josiah proclaimed the plan of God for my life, which was to not give up until the inner dragon of my negative thoughts was entirely dead and the power of the enemy who opposed me through my thought life was silenced!

Pray this prayer:

Thank you Lord, that You will move heaven and earth to connect with me. You are for me and not against me. You have incredible plans for me, to mature me and lead me to become more like You. Thank You for your faithfulness to me and to our relationship. I yield and trust that no matter what I am going through right now, You are for me. Help me to find rest in my life and teach me how to be still. I love you, Lord. Amen.

Activation #1:

If you haven't been out in nature for a while, go sit in the stillness of a forest, or by a lake, or in a park somewhere: just sit in the beauty and quiet of nature. Nothing amazing has to happen there. Take time to look around you and appreciate the beauty all around you. Breathe deeply and admire God's handiwork. Let it bring rest to your soul.

Activation #2:

Remind yourself of the good things God is doing in your life right now. Bring the difficult things to Him in conversation and tell Him exactly how you feel, but start and end with thankfulness about the good things He's done and is doing. If you struggle with being negative, don't give attention to your mental storyteller. Instead, practice thankfulness for all the times in the past and present where He has been faithful. Do this each day for a few weeks, and don't give up until the dragon of negativity is dead!

Activation #3:

Consider whether you get enough sleep. If not, dialogue with God about what needs to change in order to honor your body and move toward healthy choices of rest.

Takeaway:

Sleep is not just a secondary part of our lives; it's a gift from God to reset our spirit, soul, and body. There is another kind of rest that comes from trust in God, a rest that enables us to be still in every storm. We get to take part in pursuing that calming rest by bringing our thoughts into alignment with thankfulness and focusing on what God IS doing, rather than what He isn't doing.

CHAPTER 9

RECALIBRATION

"God is the friend of silence. See how nature—trees, flowers, grass—grows in silence; see the stars, the moon, and the sun, how they move in silence." [1] – Mother Theresa

We have an Italian espresso machine with an accompanying coffee bean grinder. I've noticed on days when the temperature outside is either hot or cold, I need to change the size of the grind. Depending on the humidity of the air, which is affected by ambient temperature, the espresso machine pulls the shot differently. I spoke with a friend in the coffee business that affirmed this point. He added that he recalibrates his coffee grinders several times throughout each day in order to compensate for the rising or dipping of external and internal temperatures.

Recalibrate means *to correct, to adjust, to reexamine (one's thinking, a plan, a system of values, etc.) and correct it in accord with a new understanding or purpose.* [2] <u>In our context, to recalibrate means to **correlate our being with heaven's atmosphere or standard.**</u> Like adjusting a coffee grinder throughout the day for a quality cup of java, it will benefit us to stop and recalibrate our lives throughouteach day: to tune in with God and remember who we are as His child, seated in heavenly places (Ephesians 2:6). We need both God and other people to help us in that process of spirit and soul recalibration. We need those who will say to us when we speak out of line, "Hey, what you said was not okay." We need them to help lead us back to truth and to healing.

When I was in my twenties my friend nicknamed me, *Three-steps-too-far-Kornaros.* I would say a lot of things without considering who I was hurting or how extreme my statements were. I wanted to be real and speak the truth without holding back. There were many times (and occasionally, there are still times) that I had to go back and apologize to someone for not being aware of or sensitive to their feelings. My insensitivity as a young adult was unloving. Part of maturing meant learning when to hold my words and bring them to God alone and how to use my words to speak life. I needed some serious help to recalibrate and move toward living my life in heaven's atmosphere!

Recalibrating Is Intentional

There is no formula to recalibration. It may be that other people remind me to take the higher road as a citizen of heaven. In chapter ten we'll talk more about how God speaks to us through people, to communicate His grace and love, and also to call us to recalibrate, grow, and mature as people.

A lot of recalibration happens when I'm alone as I interact with God, or I just need to take a breather. It depends on the day, situation, or the life experience I encounter as to what form it takes. Sometimes I simply have to stop what I'm doing and talk to my wife or go lie down on my recliner and connect with God. At other times, I hop in my truck and go for a drive. Even pulling up a hilarious video online can help me recalibrate as I remind myself to laugh! Recalibration can be as easy as grabbing a cold glass of lemonade or going for a therapeutic run. Having said all that, my recalibration will differ from yours, because, as I said, there is no formula.

Recalibrating is daily, and it's WORK. Nothing of worth ever comes without paying a price. Renewing your DMV license is work; renewing your passport is work; renewing your mind is work. Recalibration of your spirit and soul is work. The Bible talks about *offering yourselves as a living sacrifice* and *being transformed by the renewing your mind* (Romans 12:1,2); *bringing a sacrifice of praise* (Hebrews 13:15); and *God training my hands for war and my fingers for battle* (Psalm 144:1). These phrases all involve *effort*. Read them again and notice words like *offering, sacrifice, renewing,* and *being trained*. These words speak of making intentional choices. In order to grow and mature as believers, we need to put in time and energy to recalibrating our beings. The end results are well worth it.

How much time do you spend recalibrating your spirit and soul to align with who you are as a son or daughter of God? What are you putting in your mind? What do you do in your free time? It may help to think of it in terms of a diet. If you live on a diet of fast food, you're bound to have stomach problems. What goes in will impact your body. It's no different in the spiritual realm. How much time do you spend building up your soul and recalibrating your heart, your mind, and your spirit? God will not read your Bible for you. But if you make time and are intentional, He will inspire you and speak to you through it. When you pick up your Bible and quiet your soul, pressing into Him relationally, He'll meet you there.

Carving out a Place

One of my friends sold his home and moved into a fifth wheel with his family. He shared with me that in his new living situation he was having a difficult time finding a place to be alone and pray. I told him when my home is loud, I head out to my truck. He caught the idea and did the same by sitting in his car in the early mornings to pray and find his place of peace.

Situations may not always be ideal. Sometimes we may need to carve out a place to be alone in order to recalibrate and reengage with who we are as that new creature in Christ (2 Corinthians 5:7). I've discovered some interesting places in the middle of my home and family where I can grab a bit of alone time. When my kids are being loud during playtime, I often hide in the bathroom for a few minutes. I turn on the fan and find my quiet, still space. My wife will ask me as I pass by, "Are you going to have fan time?" I laugh about it, but the bathroom is a sacred space. I need to write a book called *The Sacred Space: Stories of Bathroom Epiphanies*. In the movie, Back to the Future, the character named Doc hits his head in the bathroom and comes up with the invention of a Flux Capacitor for his time machine. Come on people, it's genius!

At the moment while I write, I'm sitting in the laundry room with the fan on and the dryer running. My kids are dancing to music upstairs. It's the quietest place I could find to drown out noise in order to think. Finding space and time to be alone and recalibrate isn't always easy, but it is almost always possible.

The Pattern of the Gospel

Romans 12:2 says, "Be not conformed to the pattern of this world." I pondered that statement and asked myself, "What *is* the pattern of the world, anyway?" Was there a pattern in Paul's time that correlates to today's culture? It was when I read the rest of the chapter that I understood the answer.

Here are some phrases from the following verses in Romans 12 (capitalization mine):

- Verse 3: Don't self-promote. Find your VALUE in God, not in people or things.
- Verses 4-5: We are part of a community/body of Christ. Our ACTIONS don't just affect us.
- Verses 6-8: You have a gift. Use it to SERVE those around you.
- Verses 9, 21: HATE EVIL, LOVE GOOD.
- Verses 10,13-20: LOVE GOD, LOVE PEOPLE. Do to others, as you would have them do to you.

These verses reveal the *pattern of the world* versus the *pattern of the gospel*. The world's pattern is *ME-centered*, focused on what I can *get* out of life. But the pattern of the gospel is *US-centered*, focused on what I can *give* to God and those around me. This is why Paul writes that we're to be transformed and renewed from thinking of only ourselves to thinking of others.

God brings the transformation of our souls and spirits through those quiet places and spaces where we stop each day and recalibrate, where we pull into Him with our questions, our hearts, and our friendship. The transformation in us happens as we build a connection with God, and through His love for us, we then build loving connections with people. Recalibration happens when we pull into who we are in heaven, day after day, month after month, year after year as we are slowly becoming transformed. We become loving, US-centered humans who *recognize* we're deeply loved, and who enjoy giving away the love we've received. That is the priceless, eternal value of intentional, daily recalibrations. Go ahead, and...

...Take a moment right now. Connect with the love of your life, with God. Everything else can wait. Nothing is more important than connection—NOTHING. Allow yourself to be transformed by His presence.

Pray this prayer:

Father, thank You for Your love, Your peace, and Your friendship. I yield and surrender to You right now. Draw me deeper into Your presence, Your trust, and Your friendship. I love You Lord. Amen.

Activation #1:

How do you recalibrate throughout each day? Pay attention to what works or what has worked in the past. Lean into that and do it regularly.

Activation #2:

If you find yourself angry or upset or not acting like your true self, ask yourself a simple question: "Why am I acting this way?" Ponder that question in a quiet moment. You will probably be able to recognize how it began. You can then invite the Lord in to bring healing, cleansing, and recalibration to your true, new-creation self.

Takeaway:

We are heavenly creatures with a new DNA. Each day, we can correlate our being with who we are in heaven. It requires intentional and deliberate recalibration. We do that daily, sometimes by pulling away to be with God for a few moments, and at other times by simply taking a moment to refresh in a way that is meaningful for us.

CHAPTER 10

GOD SPEAKS THROUGH PEOPLE

"All profound things, and emotions of things, are preceded and attended by silence." [1] – Herman Melville

Countless times, God has broken the mold of how I thought He could speak to me. He has communicated to me through anyone and everyone; through those who gave me a word of wisdom, through friends, clients, grocery store checkers, and through many other people. His name is *the Word,* and He is always speaking (John 1:1).

God will often use others to draw us to Him. As we develop the habit of listening actively, we will recognize when God is communicating through people—because we've learned how to listen for and identify His voice. So when He speaks through what people around us are saying, we'll discern that God is using their words to communicate to us.

He uses people to open our eyes to His ways and His heart. And He will use them to call us deeper into relational transparency and vulnerability, because He is aware that we live in a world where sin can cause us to close ourselves off to deep connections with Him.

Before Katie came into my life, I knew deep in my heart there was someone out there I would eventually marry: someone I would fall in love with who would become my wife. But I chose to keep myself distracted until that "someone" came along. I wanted the good feelings and fun of dating without doing any work to build true intimacy. As a result, much of my dating experience did little more than stroke my ego and keep me from feeling alone. But my choices only created more pain for me and others. I was trying to fill a deep need through relationships, but without any of the commitment or vulnerability.

When I was nineteen I asked God, "Where is my wife from?" I saw these words in my mind: *New Zealand*. I thought, *when will I ever meet someone from there?* And I asked myself, *who would believe me if I told them I saw that in my spirit?*

Thirteen years later, it happened. My wife Katie is from New Zealand, and the only woman I ever had a real *peace* about dating. There was very little stress and it was easier than I could have imagined. In fact, it was the first time I could be myself in a dating relationship. I also felt God's favor over the relationship, which made it so much easier to navigate.

God had directed my path to the one He saw for my future, to the one who would be my marriage partner. I didn't know it at the time, but Katie would also become God's voice of communication to me, calling me to restoration so He could bring out the best in me.

In a minute, I'll share how God used Katie to speak to me about my need for further healing. But first I want to share how God also spoke to my grandfather Paul about his wife (my grandmother) being from another country (in the same way He spoke to me about Katie being from New Zealand). God then used Paul to communicate to his future wife about her need to receive Jesus as her Savior.

My grandfather Paul's testimony of meeting my grandmother Mary is none other than miraculous! He was 48 years old in the 1930s when he prayed, "God, is it in Your will for me to be married?" He went to sleep that night and had a dream of a woman. In the dream, God said to him, "Go to your hometown and find her." At the time Paul was living in the United States. His hometown was on the island of Crete in Greece.

In faith, he took the three-week-long ship ride back to his hometown. When Paul dropped into a café in the port city of Chania, Crete, he made a new friend. Dimitri introduced himself to Paul because he'd noticed his clothing looked different than the attire worn by the locals. It had made him curious as to why Paul was in the café. Kind-hearted Dimitri then invited Paul to stay at his house before he continued on in his journey.

Upon meeting Dimitri's family Paul recognized Dimitri's sister Mary as the woman he'd seen in his dream! But Mary was engaged to be married to another man—a man who did not treat her well, a man who was having affairs even during their engagement.

Paul was perplexed. For several days, he spent time praying in the backyard. He said to God, "If Mary is to be my wife, the sign for me will be that she becomes a Christian, is filled with the Spirit, and accepts my proposal."

A few days later, Mary came outside where Paul was praying. She said to him, "I have been watching you out here every day. Who are you talking to, and why are you emotional?" Paul answered, "I talk to God and spend time with Him, and He brings me joy." Mary responded, "I want what you have." That day, she accepted Jesus as her Savior, was filled with the Spirit, and accepted my grandfather's marriage proposal!

My grandfather didn't know it at the time, but a few months prior, Mary had prayed a desperate prayer to God. She'd said to Him, "God, if you're real, send me a man who loves me. I don't care if he looks like a monkey."

God heard my grandmother Mary's desperate plea.

He heard my grandfather's intentional prayer about marriage. He sent my grandfather across the ocean to answer the cry of my grandmother. He led Dimitri into the café to strike up a conversation with Paul and put it on his heart to invite him to his home. God used people in orchestrating each aspect of these Divine answers to prayer. His works are vast, far beyond what we can imagine! And by the way, my grandmother got quite a catch, since Grandfather was quite a handsome man!

God Speaks Through Katie

God used my grandfather in speaking to my grandmother about salvation. He used Katie to communicate to me about my need for further healing. In particular, He put His finger on the need for healing of soul-wounds from my past. While we were dating, Katie said to me, "If we are going to get married, you need to first work through some of your issues." She was particularly blunt because she wasn't willing to walk into a marriage where she would need to work things out for me in order for us to have a quality relationship. She wanted to enter our marriage knowing I'd put in the work to get healthy so our marriage could be healthy.

God was communicating to me through my future wife! I knew I had some broken areas in my life that needed fixing. And if it hadn't been for the goal of getting married, I probably would not have faced those issues. At one point I even considered breaking off the relationship with Katie rather than face some painful issues hiding beneath the surface in my soul. But I knew our relationship was well worth any discomfort I might face while dealing with my *stuff*. Dating Katie was the first time I'd chosen a relationship that would sharpen me and make me a better person.

I've shared about our dating relationship for two reasons. First, to illustrate that God often speaks to us through other people. If we've learned to recognize His voice, we'll discern His messages through their voices. Secondly, I've shared in order to bring the discussion full circle, back to our relationship with God.

Through Katie's honest words, God was showing His love for me. Through her, God called me toward healing so I could have greater intimacy with Him, with her as my wife, and with others. He loved me too much to let me stay in the places of wounding that hindered my relational connections.

In the past I'd often kept God at a distance. I'd made Him my backup plan in case my plans didn't work. I'd also done this with people because it was difficult for me to trust others. Leaders and friends had hurt me. As a result, I'd closed off my heart to people and to God so no one could hurt me again.

If you're willing to put the time and effort into knowing Him and being known by Him, He will put in the work to build a relationship with you! God is a good Father. He draws you to Himself and speaks to you in your times of silent connection. He also speaks through your friends and family, coworkers, and through strangers. Listen for His voice.

The longer Katie and I are married, the better we are getting at helping each other by speaking the truth in love. When my wife senses I'm stressed or I sense she is stressed, we ask simple questions like, "I noticed you snapping at me/the kids/the cat, etc. Are you okay? Do you need a few minutes alone?"

At times when I've made certain comments about a situation or a person, Katie has lovingly responded, "Chris, you need to deal with that because you've mentioned it several times this week, and it's obvious that person hurt you." My close friends have done the same by speaking truthfully and calling me toward a higher, better choice. Katie and my friends are often God's voice, helping me to move toward my true identity as a son of God.

Loving Confrontation

It's only natural that we can also be wounded by the words of others. Rather than shoving down hurts or offenses until they're buried in our subconscious soul, we can take time to sit back in silence or solitude to ponder them. If we stuff down our offense or hurt, we can't expect anything to change or for healing to automatically manifest. We must do some digging, prayer, and heart reflection. We may need to come to a place of forgiveness of others (or ourselves) and with God's help, drop our offenses and bless those involved.

But there are times when prayer and pondering with God about a relational struggle will only take us so far. After the reflection and digging process has finished, we may actually need to *do* something about our wound or offense. We may need to *confront the person*. Confronting in anger is like pouring gas on a fire. Confronting in love is a thousand times easier. The end goal of any confrontation should always be love.

Confrontation was once explained to me in a clear and simple format called *The Sandwich*. When confronting someone, we wrap the words of confrontation inside honest, loving statements spoken just prior to and after our confrontational words.

The first layer of the *confrontation sandwich* is to check in with the person and let them know you care. You could encourage them and tell them why you appreciate them and express that you value their friendship. Second, share the *meat* of the sandwich (the details about the area that has caused pain or hurt), always using non-accusing language. For example, use 'I' language…as in, "When you said X, I felt Y," or "When you did A, I was hurt because it reminded me of B." Don't use accusing language like, "You hurt me" or "My pain is your fault." In your communication, own your feelings and communicate what the other person did, but don't place the responsibility for your feelings on them. Finally, in the third and last layer of the communication sandwich, finish the conversation with words that show you respect them, care for them, and love them.

Honor should be part of confrontation, whether you're doing the confronting or whether someone is confronting you. You deserve respect and honor, as all people deserve respect and honor. If you were raised in a culture or community where you felt your voice was not heard or validated, you need to learn that your voice is important, and your words are important.

If you confront in love and your friends don't respect you for it, then find friends who *will* respect you. Writer and speaker John Eldredge says, "Let people feel the weight of who you are and let them deal with it."[2] This quote is *not* a license to say hurtful things. Eldredge is encouraging you to speak what's in your heart without worrying about what people will think, say, or feel. It means when you speak, BE YOU, because people will respect your honest individualism.

Proverbs 27:5-6 (TPT) says: "It's better to be corrected openly if it stems from hidden love. You can trust a friend who wounds you with his honesty, but your enemy's pretended flattery comes from insincerity." True friends will help us grow through loving confrontation, but they will do so with sincere hearts out of respect. If our friends don't respect us, we may need to respond by lovingly confronting them about their disrespect or dishonor. If they don't hear us, we may need to set boundaries and move on from the relationship as God directs. Please hear me in this, I am not talking about leaving a close friendship and certainly not a covenant relationship like a marriage because we don't feel heard.

If you (or your spouse) have been raised in dysfunctional home environments, you might need help in learning healthy communication skills. You may also need to be taught about honor and healthy boundaries in relationships. If you need help, don't hesitate to pursue learning new ways of good communication that are life-giving, non-threatening, and honoring of each person's worth. Learning new skills is well worth it. The payoff is healthy, peaceful, and honoring relationships.

We need each other. It's essential to be real with God and to also learn to be real with trusted people who will speak the truth to us in love. The stress and anxiety we experience when we're not vulnerable can cripple us and also blind us to seeing areas of our lives where we need growth or change. This type of vulnerability is one reason Alcoholics Anonymous and similar types of groups exist—for people like us to share and speak out our hurt and pain. As the lyrics of the band DC Talk express so aptly in their song, "Between You and Me," *Confession is the road to healing.*

Pray this prayer:

Jesus, I want to know your voice more than any other voice. Help me hear when You are speaking and help me respond quickly. Give me increasing wisdom to know when you're communicating to me through people. I want to connect with you at a deeper level. Teach me your ways. I love you, Lord. Amen.

Activation #1:

Think about a time when a person spoke to you, and you sensed it was God's voice communicating through them. Did it line up with God's Word? How did you receive it? What was God expressing to you through that person's words? Thank God for His desire to communicate to you. Express your gratitude to Him for His faithfulness to pursue you with His love.

Activation #2:

Spend time with Him. Learn to discern how he speaks and become familiar with His voice. Dialogue with Him.

Sit in silent connection with Him. And when He calls you deeper through healing and restoration, be courageous. It's worth the effort! What is He speaking to you in this season? Are you listening?

Takeaway:

God speaks to us in the quiet place. He also speaks to us through other people who help us grow into maturity and lovingly confront when needed. Honor should be part of confrontation. We may need to learn new skills for communication, but the payoff is healthy, peaceful relationships.

CHAPTER 11
SILENCE IS GOLDEN

"Speech is silver, silence is golden."[1] – Thomas Carlyle

Silence That Phone

Why do movie theaters display the phrase, *Silence your cell phones* across the movie screen prior to the start of the movie? The reason is, everyone knows what it's like to have a movie interrupted when another moviegoer answers their ringing phone and talks out loud while the movie is in progress. It disrupts all those nearby.

I bought a cell phone when they were first released in the 1990s. Soon after I purchased it, I volunteered for our church youth program at an onsite coffee shop. In order to help make drinks and serve customers, I put my phone away. During my break I looked for my phone and couldn't find it. For the next two hours I searched, to no avail, and started freaking out about its disappearance.

What bothered me most was not that I might need to replace a lost phone. I was worried about one of my friends trying to call or text me, and my not responding to them in time. I was afraid of missing out on my social life as a twenty-five-year-old.

That day I made a silent, unspoken vow to never again be a slave to my cell phone. To this day (twenty years later), I don't like my phone. Yes, it's a necessary tool that helps me function in life more efficiently, but I do not love it. Nor do I ever want it to rule over me. Yes, it has cool things that help me get things done. But it can also distract me, like video games distracted me as a teenager. We all need to hold cell phones and other media-related devices with open hands and not let them govern our lives.

Some of our friends have chosen to manage their phone use. Others have chosen to simplify. My wife and I have a friend who decided to forego having a phone with Internet, apps, and email. She wanted a less complicated life and told my wife, "I can always check my email on my computer and I was just wasting my time on my apps and on the Internet." So now she owns a phone that can only be used to call and text others. Another friend confessed to me he wanted to switch to a simpler phone but enjoyed his phone's instant social media connections too much to take that step.

Whether you're one who decides to opt for a simpler phone or stay with a smartphone, the question is; are you able to put it down and rest from it for a while? Because of work requirements you may not have the luxury of using a simpler phone. But you *do* have the choice to put it down and walk away from it during your personal time.

Television, Media, And Advertising

I am fond of so many of the stories my mom told us while we were growing up. One of my favorites was about her father (my grandfather Paul, whose story I shared in the previous chapter). When television first became available for people to purchase, Paul asked God, "Lord, what do you think about me buying a television?" That same night he had a dream about snakes going in and out of the television and slithering all around it. He had his Divine answer. The interpretation of the dream was obvious to him: television would release darkness into his life and family.

Yes, there are God-breathed viewing options being shown on television these days. But there is also a stream of chaos, distraction, and evil flowing out of televisions into living rooms all over the world. A few years ago my wife and I made the decision to remove ourselves and our family from exposure to too much television. We no longer wanted the battle of filtering out what was shocking from what was acceptable. And since shows and advertising often push the limit of what's acceptable, we felt it wasn't worth our time and energy to have to censor everything. We still have a television, but we only play movies and cartoons that have limited advertisements or none at all. Currently our television is in its box, sitting in our garage in storage.

Let's face it, we've become numb to the number of advertisements that bombard us daily. Ads are influencing and forming our decision-making all the time: printed media in the mail, billboards along the road, ads on our phones, ads on social media, and even suggestions given by friends.

My wife has commented that she is a marketer's dream because she gets sucked into purchasing items that use clever or quality advertising. One Christmas she purchased all my Christmas presents from Instagram ads that popped up in her Instagram feed. Her gifts were all great tools I have since used, but if she hadn't been bombarded with ads for them, not one of them would've come my way at Christmas.

Things can, and often do, lead us away from intimacy. There are things that can dull our spiritual desire and sensitivity and distract us and keep us numb from what is on God's heart. They can keep us from experiencing deep relationships with the Trinity. These *things* can keep us from the golden silence that our spirits, souls, and bodies so desperately need.

The root issue of consumerism and its hold on humans is well explained by Author Richard Foster, who writes:

Because we lack a Divine Center, our need for security has led us into an insane attachment to things...we crave things we neither need, nor enjoy... we are made to feel ashamed to wear clothes or drive cars until they are worn out. Until we see how unbalanced our culture has become at this point, we will not be able to deal with the mammon spirit within ourselves, nor will we desire Christian simplicity. [2]

Music, movies, social media, cell phones, the computer, and digital *things* are all tools we use for business or entertainment. In their own right, none of these are negative. But we *must* train ourselves to handle them wisely. We can use them to our advantage, but they can also use us to their advantage. Massive amounts of our time are wasted on various devices, when we could be using that time much more productively.

Statistically Speaking

The Bureau of Labor Statistics has been documenting data for twenty years on the *American Time Use Survey*. According to their 2020 statistics the average American has 5.5 hours of leisure time at their disposal daily:

The average American spends 22 minutes a day participating in sports, exercise, and recreation; 32 minutes per day socializing or communicating; and 26 minutes per day relaxing or thinking. In contrast, they spend 211 minutes per day watching TV. That's 2.6 times more time watching TV than exercising, relaxing, and socializing combined. [3]

The article goes on to state that people who use social media are, in fact, the most socially isolated; and heavy TV watching is tied to lower levels of satisfaction in life. The ultimate goal of the article is to encourage heavy media users to examine how their time is spent and to challenge them to consider replacing some media time with healthy activities or positive social interactions. They call it *social economizing* and add, "It's okay to be dependent on your phone. But when it starts interfering with your life rather than helping you to live a better one, you need to shift." [3]

You'll be glad to learn, as I did from this article, there is a *Screen Time* setting on many smartphones that tracks overall phone usage, as well as which apps you're using and for how long you use them: a highly beneficial tracking device if you want to cut back on phone usage.

We need time to rest and relax, and we all find different ways to do so. But there is a difference between resting and relaxing and doing activities that are enjoyable. For example, fun activities we participate in could actually create in us a deeper need for rest. Let's say I go to a movie theater for some chill time, but what I really need to do is to put on some quiet music and settle my mind.

In the end, I might come away from the movie theater feeling more stressed than before I left home.

We can cram our schedule with more events because we think they'll make us feel happier and more fulfilled. But in reality, *less* is often *more* in terms of activity and our choices for entertainment. If we can learn to value *quality* over *quantity* in terms of choosing what we do with our time, we'll be more rested and fulfilled.

The Gold In Silence

Silence is Golden is a well-known phrase that compares the value of silence to the value of gold. If we saw *silence* as a precious commodity, we might value it more highly.

As a result of the shutdowns in 2020, policy measures affected all of society, including schools. As a result, our elementary-age kids were homeschooled and spent all day at home. On some of those days, silence was worth its weight in gold to me!

Gold is priced and valued using five different determiners: gold futures price, gold spot price, supply and demand, market conditions, and currency depreciation. [4]

Let's look at each of these and apply them to the value of silence:

Gold has a *future price* because of the delivery of a specified amount of gold you want on a set date in the future.

Spot price is purchasing it and getting it delivered to you immediately.

Supply and demand: when gold is in high demand and there are limited amounts available, the price goes up.

Market conditions affect the price in relation to how the economy is doing.

Currency depreciation: Gold prices tend to maintain or appreciate in value, but the dollar can go up or down. If the dollar goes down, it will cost more to buy gold. If the dollar goes up in value, gold prices increase as well.

When gold is in limited supply, we'll pay more for it. How much will we give for silence if it's in limited supply? If we have a small amount of quiet time to ourselves, silence will appreciate in value. Or, if we desperately need silence, we may be willing to pay a hefty *spot price,* like promising to do someone else's chores for a week in exchange for that peace and quiet. We pay a *future price* for silence by reserving future hours on our calendar that create space for solitude. In doing so, we're protecting our upcoming schedule from the crush of busyness and building into our lives a rhythm of rest and refreshment. The payoff is a saner schedule with lots of emotional and spiritual benefits.

For the sake of illustration, imagine for a moment that your co-workers and your boss are your roommates. You see them at work; you come home to them; you do life with them 24/7, day in and day out. In this scenario, you would treasure alone time, wouldn't you? What effort would you make to find a space all to yourself?

The point is, media and events will always be calling for our attention and our time. The temptation is real to fill every moment by scrolling through our phones, listening to a podcast, or turning on the television. And access to distraction is constant: as easy as pushing a button.

Silence—time spent in quiet reflection or stillness—is a *necessary, essential* part of experiencing a peace-filled, God-connected life. Don't let the distractions of media and technology steal from your opportunities for silence. Make changes to your life as needed by putting away technology, saying "No" to events or activities that aren't your best choice, and pressing into the silence. You'll discover it truly is golden.

Silence is a rare commodity. If you value it in the present and plan for it in the future, it'll add wealth to the spiritual and emotional aspects of your life. Value silence and prioritize it. You'll be glad you made that choice!

Pray this prayer:

Jesus, help me let go of the unnecessary things that are vying for my attention. I don't need distractions in my life. I need more of you. May I hate the things that You hate and love the things that You love. I love You, Lord. Amen.

Activation #1:

Try cutting out an activity for one week. See if you respond positively to it.

Activation #2:

Take an assessment of your spare time. How much of it is wasted time? Could you be using your time more effectively to fulfill the dreams and goals of your heart? Write down some goals that define what you want to accomplish in your life. Those goals will help keep you on track and prevent you from wasting time and energy on diversions that have little or no value.

Takeaway:

Media and technology are prime distractions in life. They tend to pull us away from God's priority for us, which is relational time with Him and a rested life. If we see silence as a precious commodity, we'll recognize that silence is, in fact, golden, and valuable for our wellbeing and our relationship with God.

CHAPTER 12
LINGERING WITH GOD

"Why hurry over beautiful things? Why not linger and enjoy them?"[1] – Clara Schumann

During our engagement and in the early years of our marriage, Katie and I had multiple conversations centered around the book called *The Five Love Languages*, by Gary Chapman. We both wanted to understand how our financé/spouse felt most loved. Katie mentioned *quality time*, one of the love languages, was her priority. I asked her to explain what quality time looked like to her. She said, "I like it when we are both sitting together in the same room." I responded with, "That's it? Okay, that's awesome. I can do that!"

Lingering with God is like that: being present together with no agenda, and sometimes, without even a need to talk. Lingering with God is a mindful knowing that God is present with you, and you are with Him.

I love watching couples, or even friends, hanging out on rocking chairs on a porch. It gives me the sense that this is the way life is supposed to be lived and enjoyed; hanging out with the ones we love, with no agenda, with nowhere to be, and nothing to do but to be together. I want my conversations with God to be like those relational porch times.

One definition states that lingering is, "To be slow in parting or in quitting something." The first amusing thought that comes to mind with regard to *quitting something* is the making of New Year's resolutions. Such a large percentage of people give up on their resolutions by the month of February: 80%, to be exact. A high percentage of people's goals of working out, eating better, being kinder, taking up a new hobby, or any number of other resolutions, end up being forgotten because of distraction, interruption, or lack of resolve. [2]

New Year's resolutions I've made in past years have been mostly overbearing and too difficult to achieve. The reason for that was my focus on short-term benefits rather than a long-term view of what I'd hoped to achieve. An article I read helped me understand it's important to determine *why* I want to accomplish a particular goal, and that I needed to make those goals *measurable* in order to succeed. [3]

In our times with God, if we know *why* we want to meet with Him and we set *measurable goals*, we'll be more likely to experience success. Why do we want to meet with God? What does success look like? When I talk and pray to God, I measure success by **knowing I've connected with Him.** When I perceive that I've opened up my heart to Him and have been open to listening to Him communicate to me, I know I've accomplished my goal.

That measurable goal of true connection with God can be satisfied through various means, like reading the Bible, praying, reading a daily devotional, dialoguing with God, or by all of the above. The goal is to connect with God, but the pathway to that connection can look very different. *What matters is that my heart meets God's heart.*

Lingering Without Agendas

It's when we come to meet God and have an agenda that we may find it difficult to linger. We need to remember, our goal is *connection* with God and not *results* with God. We've all experienced times when prayer or reading the Bible or doing the right Christian things have seemed like a chore. When these feel like work or become so repetitive that we lose interest, that's the time to put on the brakes and return to our goal of heart-to-heart connection.

Sometimes I inadvertently come to God with an agenda of, "Hurry up and speak to me so I can move on with my day." But if I approached a close friend or a spouse in that way, I would have some relational messes to clean up with them! When we don't hear or feel something in the allotted time we've set aside for God to speak to us, it could be that we've set an agenda for Him to speak within a certain time frame or in a certain way. But God wants to meet us relationally, not according to an agenda.

Nor do we want to go to God just to get something from Him. As an example, allow me to share a vulnerable moment from my life and my relationship with God. Once, only seconds after being intimate with my wife, I heard God speak to my heart, *You come to Me for a quickie, but you don't stay for intimacy.* I knew in my spirit God was telling me, "You come and spend time with Me for a quick revelation. You come so I can show you something cool, something amazing. But you don't want to spend time with Me as a friend." This has been a deeply convicting eye-opener in my prayer life. I never want to use God as a slot machine.

We all know the story of Martha and Mary, where Martha is in the kitchen making dinner preparations and Mary is sitting at Jesus' feet. It's an account from Jesus' life that highlights His view of busyness and distraction and the greater priority of lingering with Him. Through Luke's sharing of the incident, we get the revelation that Jesus loves when we linger. It's a priority for Him, so it needs to be a priority for us.

As Jesus and the disciples continued on their journey, they came to a village where a woman welcomed Jesus into her home. Her name was Martha, and she had a sister named Mary. Mary sat down attentively before the Master, absorbing every revelation he shared. But Martha became exasperated with finishing the numerous household chores in preparation for her guests, so she interrupted Jesus and said, "Lord, don't you think it's unfair that my sister left me to do all the work by myself? You should tell her to get up and help me."

The Lord answered her, "Martha, my beloved Martha. Why are you upset and troubled, pulled away by all these many distractions? Mary has discovered the one thing most important by choosing to sit at my feet. She is undistracted, and I won't take this privilege from her." Luke 10: 38-42 (TPT)

Did Martha have a task to finish? Yes. Was she doing anything wrong? No. To be fair, Martha felt overwhelmed and was upset that her sister wasn't helping her. But Jesus pulled out a greater point. He said, "Martha, you are distracted." This is the greater revelation.

I spoke with a God-loving friend recently at the end of a church service. He mentioned that during the worship time he'd found it difficult to hear and focus on God.

He told me, "I was too distracted with what I have to do this week." He added, "I don't hear God's voice," to which I replied, "You *do* hear God's voice. You just have a lot going on right now and you need to learn how He speaks to you and how you sense His communications."

Like Martha, if we aren't giving God enough opportunity to speak to us through times of silence, it may be because we're *distracted* or *too busy*. This is one reason He has to speak to us in dreams or wake us up in the middle of the night to speak to us, when our souls are quieted enough to pay attention.

Martha was distracted and, fair enough, she had guests. Who wouldn't be distracted with preparations for hosting? Katie and I love to host people at our home. We understand the conflict for Martha in this situation.

Jesus didn't say Martha's preparations weren't important. He revealed that Mary *chose what was most important* by sitting at His feet and listening to Him, by lingering with Him. Martha invited Jesus into her home. She knew having Him there was important. And yet, she was distracted. Could she have sat at Jesus' feet for a while and then—once He was finished speaking—asked for a group effort to help her prepare? Would most of the people coming to her house have cared if it was in disarray? Yes, she could have stopped to listen during her preparations, even for a short while. Perhaps she could have multitasked by listening with her heart and simultaneously getting food ready for her guests. If Jesus said she was distracted, then maybe she needed to stop was she was doing and sit down.

Let's be honest. It's possible that Martha was jealous of her sister, who seemed to be receiving all of Jesus' attention. As a result, she may have tried to feel less inadequate about herself by pulling her sister away from Him.

In light of this story of Martha and Mary, here are some thoughtful questions. I invite you to take time to ponder these with God and let Him speak concerning His desires to just BE with you:

- Am I able to celebrate the successes of others and protect my heart from jealousy?
- Do we have to get our lives in order before we approach God?
- Do our home and lives have to look perfect to our friends and family so they think we have it all together? Who are we trying to impress?
- Do I find it difficult to sit down and listen?
- Am I always distracted? Do I ever stop to slow down?
- Am I distracted at church or during my prayer time? Why?
- What is most important to you right now?

Growing The Habit Of Lingering

It's helpful to understand that the place of deeper connection with God isn't measured by just one event. It's really measured by many life events. Growing deeper connection is like developing a workout regimen for the sake of physical health. If I approach a workout expecting instant results, I'll set myself up for frustration and failure. Building muscle strength doesn't happen in a few days. It takes weeks and months of investing time and energy to see noticeable change.

This is how we need to approach our relationship with God. If we begin to spend time with God and don't see Him moving, or we don't see immediate answers to our prayers, or our prayer times feel meaningless—we can tend to get very discouraged and come to the conclusion that nothing is working and it's not worth our investment. But we need to remember that our answers will come. Just like that regimen in the gym takes time to tone muscles, pursuing heart-to-heart connection with God over a period of time *will* bring about a significant spiritual shift in our lives.

God is always speaking to us when we read the Bible or read uplifting devotionals, and even throughout our days at work. But the concept of *lingering* goes beyond God whispering a communication to us here and there. Lingering has to do with how long I'm willing to wait when I'm seeking God for an answer. It has to do with how long I'm willing to wait for something to happen when I'm in His presence.

I was talking to God one day about the reality of yet another immense change coming up in my family's life, expressing to Him, "God, I don't know what You're doing, but I'm going to trust Your plan for my life, even if I don't understand it." That was difficult for me to say, because I have been wrestling with trust concerning that for many years. God is not in a rush to get me to *do* anything. What's important for Him is *connection, with Him and with others.* Through the years of wrestling He has been drawing me closer in trust and friendship with Him.

It reminds me of Abraham. In Genesis 26:4 God said to Abraham, "I will make your descendants as numerous as the stars in the sky and will give them all these lands, and through your offspring all nations on earth will be blessed." God wanted to bless Abraham and to bless the earth through his descendants. But God took twenty-five years to fulfill the promise of giving Abraham a son. He wasn't in a hurry. God wanted to build trust in Abraham as He walked with him through those years of waiting. Abraham never lived to see the above promise fulfilled. But His faith rose above circumstances to believe God *would* make a nation out of him.

God may relate to us in a similar manner as He did with Abraham, because He is most interested in His friendship with us. We may have promises from God that aren't yet fulfilled. He *will* fulfill them. Our part is to be connected with God and watch as His goodness unfolds those plans for our lives. He was faithful to fulfill Abraham's promises, and He is faithful to fulfill our promises!

There is a glorious reward in the waiting. You'll discover tremendous peace and relationship in that place when God comes to speak to you. Are you waiting as long as it takes? Is your mindset in prayer, *Let's hurry up and get this over with?* Or are you willing to *linger* and wait with God in silence and stillness?

Pray this prayer:

Lord, help me come to you with no agenda and be *present* with you. Amen.

Activation:

Linger. Sit with God, without an agenda, and talk and listen to Him. Try it for 10 minutes. Recognize He is with you and He is present. Be content with focusing on His presence. It might help to choose the best time of day for the least distraction. And be aware that details of life may surface. Don't let them dissuade you from your goal of being with God. If thoughts surface about something you need to do or someone you need to call or text, write down those thoughts and then immediately refocus on the One you've come to meet.

Takeaway:

Lingering with God is to stay with Him, without an agenda, setting aside the busyness of life. The measurable goal of lingering is to connect with Him and be with Him, heart to heart. It's a practice we learn and grow over time. Lingering with God in friendship causes us to trust God over the span of our lives.

CHAPTER 13

CULTIVATING INTIMACY

"The most important part of prayer is not the result it produces, but the intimacy it creates." [1] — *Kingsley Opuwari Manuel*

Father's Desire for Intimacy

While scouting out a possible move to South Carolina, our family lived for a short time at my parent's home. In the wee hours one morning my son Josiah woke up to use the restroom. As he headed back toward his room he clearly heard the phrase *I love you* whispered to his heart. I was away on a business trip at the time. The next day when I called home Josiah told me about the voice he'd heard and said it sounded just like my voice! Though I can't say for certain what the voice was all about, I sense perhaps my son needed reassurance that I was okay. And hearing a voice that sounded like mine was the Lord's way of allowing Josiah to feel my love for him while I was gone.

My son's experience is similar to the way God spoke to the prophet Samuel as a young boy, as recorded in 1 Samuel, chapter 3. While living and serving in the temple, three times during the night Samuel heard God calling out his name, "Samuel!" Each time he awoke and heard the voice, he ran to Eli the high priest, assuming he had called him.

There is an interesting correlation between my son's story and Samuel's experience. Did God speak to Samuel and make His own voice sound like Eli's voice? Did God speak to my son Josiah and make His voice sound like his earthly daddy's voice? Perhaps God uses familiar voices to speak to us because He is aware those voices are deeply intimate to us and comforting. My son has always been very aware of the supernatural, and I think this is one of God's ways of building intimacy with him.

I didn't like the idea of intimacy while growing up. It felt too soft, vulnerable, and scary. I did not have time for it, nor did I want to give it any of my attention. In my mind, intimacy was the stuff found in romance novels and Hallmark movies. My mom would occasionally turn on the TV and watch a Hallmark movie in the living room. They always felt cheesy and fake to me. I wanted no part of that. Truthfully, Hollywood is a terrible place to find intimacy, but that was my childhood reference for the concept!

Intimacy means *closeness of friendship*. Looking back now, I realize God pursued intimacy with me throughout my entire life. But His intimacy looked much different than my childish understanding of the word.

God's Presence In Me And All Around Me

Cultivating intimacy happens in many different ways. Two of the more common choices for believers are meditating on the Word of God and entering into prayer and worship. It was while attending a ministry school in 2009 that I experienced a depth of intimacy with God's presence that made me hungrier for Him than I had ever been before.

In school we had opportunities to choose our breakout classes for the afternoon sessions. One class subject that stood out to me was *Intimacy with Jesus*. I signed up for the class, knowing I could always use more intimacy with Him.

The class was not what I expected. It was a study of the ancient mystics and of the early desert fathers who lived lives of solace in the desert or in monasteries. Coupling my lack of interest in the particular subject with the teacher's monotone voice, I found myself often dozing off. It was difficult to listen and pay attention. I almost decided to stop attending.

In hindsight, the content was good content, but at the time I'd expected to be clearly motivated toward intimacy, or to be given a call to action, or to hear amazing teaching about growing in intimacy. I made the decision to go one more time and then quit attending the class. I went for my final class the following day. The time dragged on, to the point that I became agitated. I couldn't wait to get out of there! I even considered using the restroom in order to make an early escape from class. And then it happened. The teacher had us do an exercise, one that I was not prepared for but that would change my life.

She had us close our eyes and become aware of God's presence in the room. I was hesitant at first, partly because it sounded a bit like a New-Age activity. But I closed my eyes and participated. The moment I set my mind on the fact that God's presence was in the room with me, it was as if I could *feel* Him there. For five minutes we sat there in the quiet with our eyes closed, our attention focused on God's presence nearby. I was feeling the sense of Him the entire time. Then the teacher asked us to keep our eyes closed and focus on the fact that God's presence lives *inside* of us. This time I did not hesitate. And when I focused on God's presence inside of me, it was as if I could feel him there, within me.

At the time I could not think of a scripture that could back up the experience of what had just happened, but I knew it was God drawing me closer to Himself. Since then I have read in 1 John 4:13 NLT, *"And God has given us his Spirit as proof that we live in Him and He in us."* God is in us and with us, and we are in Him and with Him. His Presence is real.

Moses couldn't explain a burning bush that wasn't consumed and a voice speaking out of the bush. But he knew it was God and drew closer to it. Rather than running in fear, he approached it in awe. He set a precedent for where we are to focus: on God and His presence.

I left class that day so high on life that when I got home, all I wanted to do was lie down on my bedroom floor and be with God, to feel His presence in and around me. I put on some background music and lay down. The only thing on my mind was, *God is here, and I'm here hanging out with Him.* Time became irrelevant. Minutes became hours. The sun had set and I was still on the floor in my room. I didn't want to get up. It felt so enjoyable to be with God in quiet, in the stillness, seeking His face.

My life has changed since that day. Something was unlocked in me, something I needed in order to connect and go deeper with God. I discovered a true, real, and pure intimacy and connection I'd always wanted but had never discovered in all my years of Christianity and attending church. I discovered the Bible is full of stories of people encountering God. I wanted to encounter Him as well, in a real, active, alive, passionate, and intimate friendship with Him.

There were times before that day in class when I had met with God. But that classroom experience brought me to a greater awareness of accessing God's presence without the help of music, or being at a church meeting, or needing another external factor to connect. Those things are good and helpful, but that day I learned what Jesus learned as a Son, that I could retreat and be with the Father in a one-on-one relational time. It was a shift I needed to make to take the next step in my relationship with my Father. It was another level of deeper friendship and of closeness and trust.

This is a step I believe He's calling every one of us to take. Will we stay in a place of contentment and comfort in our faith, or will we let our deep hunger for more drive us closer?

My experiences and encounters with God will be different than the experiences of other people. It would be impossible for me to try and make a formula out of the way God communicates and then give that formula to others. The way He speaks is endlessly creative, so any set formula would soon need to be changed. Every person needs to explore their own relationship with God and trust that His love for them is so great, He will come to meet them!

As we pursue intimacy with God, our dialogues and interactions with Him will grow and change. God's personhood and character do not change, but our relationship with Him will mature, and we will find ourselves being transformed through the closeness of our friendship with God.

Pray this prayer:

God, I want to hear you speaking to me the words, "I love you." If I have been afraid of true, godly intimacy with you, please forgive me. I choose to open my heart to you. I welcome your presence in me, around me, and through me. I love you, God! Amen.

Activation:

Sit in silence for five minutes. During that time, focus only on God and His presence all *around you*. Then take another five minutes and focus only on the fact that God's presence lives *inside of you*. Allow God to draw near as you draw near to Him.

Takeaway:

God is an intimately loving Father. The goal isn't perfection, but connection with Him. He is in us and all around us. We can experience His real, tangible presence with us at all times.

CHAPTER 14
LEAVING A LEGACY

"There is something terribly wrong with a culture inebriated by noise and gregariousness." [1] *– George Steiner*

What kind of legacy do we want to leave for our children? How are we training them in their use of time? What are we teaching them about intimacy with God? Chapter 10 took a hard look at the effects media and technology has had on our lives as adults and on our relationship with God and others. This chapter focuses on the choices we need to make as parents in order to help our children discover the priority of silence and times with God.

In our home, as I've mentioned in previous chapters, when Mommy and Daddy need a break we are quick to send the kids upstairs for quiet time. It is tempting to turn the television on to serve as an *easy babysitter* for our kids. And occasionally, when we are exhausted and we don't have the energy, we will turn a movie on and let our crew watch wholesome entertainment. But as a rule, we've allowed only minimal television interaction and have instilled in our children that watching television is a reward for having quiet time, reading, or drawing.

We'll never be able to keep our children from technology altogether. Their friends will have devices, and they will find a way to watch them! We are training them while they are younger to recognize, as we often explain, "Too much TV is like too much sugar; it's not good for you." We're not teaching them to hate technology. We're not keeping them from all interaction with it. But we are teaching them balance and the value of reading or playing quietly, versus the pursuit of constant noise and distraction.

The reality is, when I have given my children access to technology and it is time to take it away, separation from the device being used comes with a lot of tears and always with a request to watch one more show or play one more game.

I wondered why their reactions have been so strong, until I found an article on the manipulation of electromagnetism. There is a patent on electromagnetic fields to use screens (TV, computer, etc.) for subliminally manipulating humans. The following is a paragraph from the article about Patent US6506148B2 titled, "Nervous

System Manipulation by Electromagnetic Fields from Monitors:"

Physiological effects have been observed in a human subject in response to stimulation of the skin with weak electromagnetic fields that are pulsed with certain frequencies near ½ Hz or 2.4 Hz, such as to excite a sensory resonance. Many computer monitors and TV tubes, when displaying pulsed images, emit pulsed electromagnetic fields of sufficient amplitudes to cause such excitation. It is therefore possible to manipulate the nervous system of a subject by pulsing images displayed on a nearby computer monitor or TV set. [2]

These tests have revealed there is intentional manipulation to keep people coming back for more, to make it difficult for them to turn off the television. Interestingly, another article claims CEOs and upper executives of the tech world are fully aware of how addictive media devices can be, so they send their children to schools that have no technology and allow minimal technology at home! [3]

As I've already mentioned in prior chapters, I played video games during my teenage and young adult years. Though I could've spent those years learning piano or doing something more life-giving and fulfilling, I sat for many hours pressing buttons attached to Nintendo, Sega

Genesis, and Xbox games. It wasn't until around age thirty that I finally understood all those games were a waste of my time! For me, they took my focus away from real life experiences and pulled me addictively into competitive and sometimes violent fake worlds.

I'm not saying all gaming is bad or wrong, but this was my personal experience.

Now my son is always asking for permission to play video games. I will do my best to teach him that too much video game time is not beneficial for him, in hopes of saving him from future regrets about wasted time. Out of my own personal experiences, I am encouraging my son to pursue activities that in the long run, will be much more beneficial and enjoyable for him. And now, with the advent of the metaverse (a network of 3D virtual worlds focused on social connection), I must be keenly prepared as a parent to understand how video usage will affect my child's upbringing.

Francis Schaeffer wrote in 1976,

Yet the possibility of information storage, beyond what men and governments ever had before, can make available at the touch of a button a man's total history...the combined use of the technical capability of listening in on all these forms of communications [telephone, cable, fax, etc.] with the high-speed computer literally leaves no place to hide and little room for privacy. [4]

We have come a long way technologically since Schaeffer penned that statement. With the advent of the Internet and cell phones, everything is now at our fingertips. And that is just one reason it is even *more vital* that we are vigilant about instilling in our kids the value for quiet times and the beauty of silence.

Enriching Activities

Another reason for setting a family policy of putting away technology is for the pursuit of other activities that can enrich my family and my children. I came from a musical family. My mom led the church choir and sang solos at church. She would practice the songs beforehand at home. I loved hearing her sing. There was always a warm presence in the room when she sang. Though I couldn't have expressed it then, I realize now the warmth I'd felt was God's presence.

My family's interests in music and sports greatly influenced my development. I want music to be a rich part of my children's upbringing because it was such a constructive part of my own childhood. And because of my fond memories and my own positive experiences with extracurricular activities, I want my children to build similar fond memories through healthy extracurricular activities that will positively influence their development.

The most important mark I can leave on earth is to give my children a better life than the life I lived. Yes, I do want to give them a shared experience of the good times I had while growing up and recreate some of that for them. I also want my children to understand that even though we live in a digital age, we do not allow it to rule us.

Building a God-Centered Legacy

In my church community, the mindset for parenting and mentoring is summed up in this statement: *"We want our ceiling to become your floor."* Concretely, this means I want my children to grow past my level of learning and experience. It's my desire that they take what I have taught them and carry it to the next level. With that in mind, I am taking responsibility to teach them all that I know and have learned, in hopes that it will guide them to make better decisions—superior decisions than I have made in the past—and to see them succeed at a greater level than I could ever achieve. This quote from an unknown author encapsulates my parenting goals: "Family Legacy—it's not what you leave TO your children, it's what you leave IN your children."

In Writing *Silence*, my hope is that no device, person, or system will ever have a captive hold on the lives of my kids. Instead, I want them to be friends of God first and foremost, and for that primary friendship to be their motivation for living the rest of their lives. With all my heart, I want to demonstrate through my own life and through our parenting what it means to live in this world and be part of it, to be involved in it, but to realize our true Center is always in God. The chief reason for limiting technology in the lives of my children is so they can experience deep connection with God; so they build a legacy of knowing Father God and being His friend; so they treasure sacred spaces of quiet and alone times; and so they pass that precious legacy on to future generations.

Steve Saint, in speaking about passing on our own story and experiences, said, "Your story is the greatest legacy that you will leave to your friends. It's the longest-lasting legacy you will leave to your heirs."[5]

That's one reason I'm writing about my personal journey with *Silence,* to share from what I've gained for the benefit of others, and for the legacy I can sow into future generations. As I was talking to God about writing this book I asked Him, "Why do you want me to write this book?" He answered, "Because it's YOUR story." Then I asked Him, "Why don't you have a famous person write it? Won't they get more sales?" He answered, "I will guide people to buy it."

I don't know whom these pages will impact, but at the very least, I am impacting myself by doing something I have never done. And when my children grow up, they will always have this book.

We often don't perceive the impact our decisions have on people. When we choose to step out in faith, past our fears and negative self-talk, there are always others watching and learning from our lives. That's the value of living our own story in front of our children!

I pray this God-centered legacy is also the chief goal of every person and every parent who reads this book. In writing about technology and the legacy we'll leave to others, it's my hope that we are successful in one primary thing: fostering intimacy with God in the lives of our children and in the lives of the next generation.

Pray this prayer:

Jesus, you are the most important person in my life. Let all the other things fall to the wayside—the things I have pursued in order to try and find my purpose, meaning, and significance. Nothing else matters more than right now, being right here with You. Draw me deeper into your love. And Father, may I pass on the legacy of my friendship with you to all those I encounter. I love you, God, and I ask this in Jesus' name. Amen.

Activation #1:

Whether or not you have children, the next generation will carry your story. Whose life are you pouring into in order to leave a legacy? How are you leaving your mark for the generations to come? If you haven't already done so, ask God to show you someone who can pour into you and help you grow; and find someone whom you can pour into and help them grow.

Activation #2:

Your past and present life choices and your future vision impact your family and friends around you. How does knowing that affect the way you will live your life from now on? Ask God for clarity, wisdom and strategy for any changes you want to make.

Takeaway:

God-centered legacies may require some changes away from technology and toward a different lifestyle. Time for enriching family activities can be one result for families who choose fewer media-centered hours. All of us will leave a mark on the next generation. What that looks like depends on our own story with God. Above all, the greatest influence we can have is to teach the next generation to walk in intimacy with God.

CHAPTER 15
JESUS AND SILENCE

"How Should We Then Live?"[1] – Francis Schaeffer

*When he (the Lamb) opened the seventh seal, there was **silence in heaven for about half an hour**. And I saw the seven angels who stand before God, and seven trumpets were given to them. Another angel, who had a golden censer, came and stood at the altar. He was given much incense to offer, with the prayers of all God's people, on the golden altar in front of the throne. The smoke of the incense, together with the prayers of God's people, went up before God from the angel's hand. Then the angel took the censer, filled it with fire from the altar, and hurled it on the earth; and there came peals of thunder, rumblings, flashes of lightning and an earthquake (Revelation 8:1-5, NIV).*

Because the book of Revelation is so cryptic, there are many interpretations as to what this passage could mean. The interpretation most scholars hold to is that through silent expectation, all of heaven is showing honor, awe, and respect to Jesus. If heaven is silent, that means the Father, the Son, the angels, the four living creatures, and the twenty-four elders are silent. All singing and worshiping has come to a halt for that half hour, and the silence of those around the throne of God has become their worship.

King David says in Psalm 65:1, 2 (TPT), "O God in Zion, to you even **silence is praise!** You who answers prayer, all of humanity comes before you with their requests."

The Amplified version beautifully expresses this same passage: "To You **belongs silence [the submissive wonder of reverence]**, and [it bursts into] praise in Zion, O God; And to You the vow shall be performed."

So what are we WAITING FOR? SILENCE is a form of WORSHIP! Let praise for Him rise as we WAIT on Him in silence!

Nothing in heaven happens without a reason. If there was worshipful silence in heaven for thirty minutes, what precedent does that set for us? While on earth Jesus taught us to pray, "Your Kingdom come, your will be done, on earth as it is in heaven" (Matthew 6:10). Is it possible this silence in heaven is something God desires for us to imitate here on earth? Is He longing for us to wait in eager expectation to see what He is going to do? Does He want us to stop and listen to Him?

All of heaven stopped and waited for Jesus for half an hour, to see what He was doing. What would it look like to stop and sit with Jesus for thirty minutes? What could happen in us? In the above scripture, right after heaven's silence, the prayers of all God's people were offered to God. What if the first thing we do when we spend time with God is to be silent before we even ask or pray anything?

Psalm 62:1 (TPT) says, "I stand silently to listen for the one I love, waiting as long as it takes for the Lord to rescue me." Other versions of this passage use phrases like, "I am at rest while waiting for Him" (NIV), or, "I wait for Him in silence" (NKJV), or, "I am waiting for him calmly" (CEV).

So we see that as our eyes are on Jesus, silence is part of our worship. As we wait quietly in His presence with anticipation and expectancy, silence is praise rising up from our heart to God in heaven. It often takes a lot to wait at rest or wait calmly in silence, but the fruit of our intentional quieting can be that our worship becomes like the atmosphere of heaven around the throne of Jesus.

Jesus' Ministry and Silence

In several scripture stories, we read about Jesus harnessing the power of silence while He walked on Earth. The apostle Matthew tells us of a dialogue between Jesus and a Canaanite woman, where Jesus uses silence to identify and draw out the heart of the woman's faith.

Matthew 15:21-28, (NIV) says:

"Leaving that place, Jesus withdrew to the region of Tyre and Sidon. A Canaanite woman from that vicinity came to him, crying out, "Lord, Son of David, have mercy on me! My daughter is demon-possessed and suffering terribly." **Jesus did not answer a word.** *So his disciples came to him and urged him, "Send her away, for she keeps crying out after us." He answered, "I was sent only to the lost sheep of Israel." The woman came and knelt before him. "Lord, help me!" she said. He replied, "It is not right to take the children's bread and toss it to the dogs." "Yes it is, Lord," she said. "Even the dogs eat the crumbs that fall from their master's table." Then Jesus said to her, "Woman, you have great faith! Your request is granted." And her daughter was healed at that moment."*

Jesus initially said nothing to this distraught woman. And when He did speak, it almost seemed as if he was turning her away. He used both His silence and His words to see how hungry she was for Him. And when she persisted and refused to give up, Jesus commended her for her faith and granted her request!

What would your faith be like if God did not answer your prayer the first time? What about the second time and the third time? Would you be discouraged?

We often give up too easily in prayer because of preconceived ideas and perceptions in how we view a circumstance, or even how we view God's response to our circumstance. We can become frustrated and discouraged when we don't get an answer within a certain time frame. If only we would keep on in our prayers and our commitment to Jesus when we receive no answers from heaven. If only we would keep asking, persisting, and waiting in silence. Our persistence will always be rewarded because God is a rewarder of those who diligently seek Him (Hebrews 11:6)!

In another scripture story, we see Jesus refusing to answer people's inquiries as part of fulfilling His earthly ministry. Let's look at Matthew 27:11-14, NIV:

> *Meanwhile Jesus stood before the governor (Pilate), and the governor asked him, "Are you the king of the Jews?" "You have said so," Jesus replied. When he was accused by the chief priests and the elders, he gave no answer. Then Pilate asked him, "Don't you hear the testimony they are bringing against you?" But Jesus*

made no reply, not even to a single charge—to the great amazement of the governor.

As the Son of Man, Jesus was the Master Negotiator, able to find the God pathway through any situation. In His conversation with Pilate, He could have walked away entirely unscathed. Yet he chose to fulfill the prophecy about his life that states, "He was oppressed and afflicted, yet he did not open his mouth; he was led like a lamb to the slaughter, and as a sheep before its shearers is silent, so he did not open his mouth" (Isaiah 53:7, NIV).

Jesus chose silence at the right time for the right purposes. He recognized the power of silence in His ministry, even silence that fulfilled His purpose as the Savior of the world intentionally walking toward the cross to bring salvation.

Jesus And You

My perception when I pray is this: *God can't wait to speak to me.*

The same is true for you. He can't wait to speak with you! He is waiting to share His secrets with you. Jeremiah 33:3, NIV, says, "Call to me and I will answer you and tell you great and unsearchable things you do not know." God wants you to come. He wants to communicate with you and to answer you. He wants to meet you in the silence.

These two verses speak of God hearing us and speaking to us; "For the eyes of the Lord are on the righteous and His ears are attentive to their prayer" (1 Peter 3:12 NIV); "My sheep hear my voice, and I know them, and they follow me"(John 10:27 ESV).

When you give Him the opportunity to come and speak; when your heart is open and you understand He is eager to communicate; when you are not put off by God's silence, but you continue to persist in waiting for Him to speak; then the possibilities are endless.

Pray this prayer:

Lord, may I have a hunger for you like the hunger of the Canaanite woman. May I persist in prayer even when heaven seems silent. Thank you that you are drawing out my heart and my hunger for you. I love you Jesus. Amen.

Activation:

Do you have any prayers you have given up praying? God has heard them all and has not forgotten you. Do you sense you need to persist in any of those prayers you have given up praying? Sometimes it takes the help of a friend to pray with us about something. Ask the Lord how to go about praying over those certain forgotten prayers, and whether you need someone to be praying with you about them.

Takeaway:

Silence is a form of worshiping Jesus. Looking into Jesus' face; watching what He is doing; observing His beauty; these are part of the stillness in heaven. May we use silence as Jesus used silence, to do the Father's will and to worship Him.

CONCLUSION

The older I become, the more I want to retreat to a quiet place where I can be with God and be still. I'm not alone in this pursuit.

Throughout time there are those who have pursued quietude to meet with God. Author Henri Nouwen writes about a significant call to silence from the pages of history: "When Arsenius, the Roman educator who exchanged his status and wealth for the solitude of the Egyptian desert, prayed, 'Lord, lead me into the way of salvation,' he heard a voice saying, 'Be silent.'" [1]

This ancient art of stillness, solitude, and silence has been around for centuries. We must rediscover its power in our present age. If we continue to choose the pathway of busyness, stress, and living in a state of being overwhelmed, we may very well lose our minds, our souls, and our Divine anchor in life.

My challenge to you is to pursue fervently the idea of

solitude and silence, whether it's a new concept for you or whether you've been familiar with it for some time. Be diligent to create YOU time, for YOU are the only one who can control your time. Be diligent to create time to pull away and be with God.

Like Jesus, let us retreat from the noise and the crowds to meet with our Father, to find peace and strength for our own lives, and to set a holy example for those who are following in our footsteps.

FOOTNOTES

Chapter 1:

1. Sarah Dessen. Just Listen. Viking, 2006.
2. Henri Nouwen. *The Way of the Heart: Connecting with God Through Prayer, Wisdom, and Silence.* New York: HarperOne, 2003. p.27.
3. Solitude definition. https://www.merriam-webster.com/dictionary/solitude
4. Stephen Palmquist, *Ontology and the Wonder of Silence, Part Four of The Tree of Philosophy* (Hong Kong: Philopsychy Press, 2000). See also, *Silence as the Ultimate Fulfillment of the Philosophical Quest, Journal Hekmat Va Falsafeh (Journal of Wisdom and Philosophy),* Issue 6 (August 2006), pp.67-76. https://en.wikipedia.org/wiki/Silence#cite_note-5
5. Rebecca Beris. Science Says Silence Is Much More Important to Our Brains Than We Think. June 2019.

https://www.lifehack.org/377243/science-says-silence-much-more-important-our-brains-than-thought
6. Atalanta Beaumont. 10 Reasons Why Silence Really is Golden. April, 2017. https://www.psychologytoday.com/us/blog/handy-hints-humans/201704/10-reasons-why-silence-really-is-golden
7. Convergence definition. https://archivemore.com/what-type-of-word-is-convergence/

Chapter 2:

1. Albert Einstein. https://www.goodreads.com/quotes/1196663-the-monotony-and-solitude-of-a-quiet-life-stimulates-the
2. Richard J. Foster, Celebration of Discipline. Harper & Row, 1978.
3. Jack Zenger & Joseph Folkman. Communication | What Great Listeners Actually Do. Harvard Business Review. July 14, 2016. hbr.org/2016/07/what-great-listeners-actually-do

Chapter 3:

1. Michael Bedard. Redwork. Stoddart, 1996.

Chapter 4:

1. Pablo Picasso. https://www.goodreads.com/quotes/629534-without-great-solitude-no-serious-work-is-possible
2. Wellable. Causes and Treatments of Leadership Burnout. October, 4, 2021. https://www.wellable.co/blog/causes-treatments-of-leadership-burnout/
3. Richard J. Foster. Celebration of Discipline. Harper & Row. 1978.
4. Maria Popova. The Art of Listening: Secrets From 17 years of Silence. April 26, 2011. https://www.theatlantic.com/entertainment/archive/2011/04/the-art-of-listening-secrets-from-17-years-of-silence/237862/

Chapter 5:

1. Blaise Pascal. https://www.goodreads.com/quotes/7490335-all-men-s-miseries-derive-from-not-being-able-to-sit
2. John Eldredge. Journey of Desire. Thomas Nelson, Inc. 2000.
3. Neil Postman. Amusing Ourselves to Death. Penguin Books. 1985.
4. Henri Nouwen. The Way of the Heart: Connecting with God Through Prayer, Wisdom, and Silence. HarperOne. 2003.

Chapter 6:

1. Charles Spurgeon. Quiet Musing No. 576. At the Metropolitan Tabernacle, Newington. https://www.spurgeongems.org/sermon/chs576.pdf

Chapter 7:

1. Franziska Spritzer. 8 Signs and Symptoms of Vitamin D Deficiency. July 23, 2018. https://www.healthline.com/nutrition/vitamin-d-deficiency-symptoms

Chapter 8:

1. Henry Wadsworth Longfellow. Delphi Complete Works of Henry Wadsworth Longfellow. Delphi Classics; 1st edition. February 5, 2013.
2. Scott, Elizabeth. The Overwhelming Benefits of Power Napping. January 2, 2020.
3. https://www.verywellmind.com/power-napping-health-benefits-and-tips-stress-3144702
4. Richard J. Foster. Celebration of Discipline. Harper & Row. 1978.

Chapter 9:

1. Mother Theresa. https://www.azquotes.com/author/14530-Mother_Teresa/tag/silence-1966 (1967).

2. Recalibrate definition. https://www.dictionary.com/browse/recalibrate

Chapter 10:

1. Herman Melville. https://www.azquotes.com/quote/606151
2. John Eldredge. Wild at Heart. Thomas Nelson, Inc. 2001.

Chapter 11:

1. Thomas Carlyle. https://www.azquotes.com/quote/947669
2. Richard J. Foster. Celebration of Discipline. Harper & Row. 1978.
3. Michelle Drouin. The Time Hack Everyone Should Know. February 4, 2022. https://thereader.mitpress.mit.edu/the-time-hack-everyone-should-know/?utm_campaign=Recomendo&utm_medium=email&utm_source=Revue%20newsletter
4. Eric Sepanek. Understanding How Gold Prices are Determined. July 12, 2017. https://www.sbcgold.com/blog/how-gold-prices-are-determined/

Chapter 12:

1. Clara Schumann. https://www.azquotes.com/quote/262655
2. CNN. December 31, 2021. https://www.abccolumbia.com/2021/12/31/research-shows-80-of-people-abandon-their-new-years-resolutions-by-february/
3. Ibid, CNN. December 31, 2021.

Chapter 13:

1. Kingsley Opuwari Manuel. https://bukrate.com/topic/prayer-quotes-quotes?p=4

Chapter 14:

1. George Steiner. Language and Silence: Essays. 1958-1966 (1967).
2. Nervous System Manipulation by electromagnetic fields from monitors. https://patents.google.com/patent/US6506148B2/en
3. Canela Lopez. 6 tech executives who raise their kids tech free or seriously limit their screen time. March 5, 2020. https://www.businessinsider.com/tech-execs-screen-time-children-bill-gates-steve-jobs-2019-9
4. Francis A. Schaeffer. How Should We Then Live? The Rise and Decline of Western Thought and Culture. Baker Publishing Group. 1976.

5. Steve Saint. https://www.azquotes.com/quote/721971

Chapter 15:

1. Francis A. Schaeffer. How Should We Then Live? The Rise and Decline of Western Thought and Culture. Baker Publishing Group. 1976.

Conclusion:

1. Henri Nouwen. The Way of the Heart: Connecting with God Through Prayer, Wisdom, and Silence. HarperOne. 2003. p.29

ACKNOWLEDGEMENTS

I read somewhere that it takes a team to write a book. Here are my Thank You's!

Thank you to all who helped beta read this book and provide feedback! Brent Cashell, Anna Tomsett, Jonathan & Brooke Huffman, and Steven Kornaros.

To my amazing proofreaders, Janet Richards, Seth Dahl, David Kornaros, Kris Rosentrater, and Isaac Harris.

Brittany Thompson, because you called out the gold in me during one of our many conversations and it helped propel me to get this manuscript off the ground.

Kris Rosentrater for coaching me through part of this process and encouraging me to see that I have more in me than I realized. For suggesting the Prayer, Activation, and Takeaway sections to be put after every chapter, and a workbook version of this book, of which I have already started and almost finished!

Naomi Specht, for editing the initial document and providing your much- needed encouragement that I was on the right track!

Janet Richards, whose interest in my book turned into a full-blown editing campaign and who helped communicate my heart into words for the reader. Thank you for hanging with me during this process. Your much needed wisdom, experience, and expertise was critical to this manuscript.

Katie, for her love and grace for all the times I interrupted her reading romance novels so I could get her feedback on a new idea, thought, or concept.

Sophia and Josiah, for being apart of this journey, and letting me share their stories with you.

To my extended family, for taking this journey with me, and allowing our stories to write these pages.

Back Cover Photo: Annique Hardin Photography

Book Jacket Design: Md Sahidul Islam Tuser

Back Cover Write up: Janet Richards, Brittany Thompson, Katie Kornaros, Chris Kornaros

Editor: Janet Richards

For contact information regarding speaking engagements and additional resources, visit us at:

CHRISKORNAROS.COM

FOLLOW CHRIS KORNAROS ON

ABOUT THE AUTHOR

Chris Kornaros desires to lead people into deeper relationship with God by providing tools to facilitate a deeper connection, sharing how God speaks to them, and enriching their time in silence and stillness. His greatest calling is to pass this message on to his children and as many people as he can. Chris has been involved in various aspects of church life for over 20 years, leading ministries involved with children, youth, worship, and small groups. Chris and his wife Katie live with their two children in Charleston, South Carolina.